EASTERN FRONT FROM F

THE WAFFEN SS
IN THE EAST 1943-1945

NICHOLAS MILTON

C✛DA
BOOKS LTD
www.codahistory.com

C⊕DA
BOOKS LTD

This paperback edition is published in Great Britain in 2011 by

Coda Books Ltd, The Barn, Cutlers Farm Business Centre,
Edstone, Wootton Wawen, Henley in Arden, Warwickshire, B95 6DJ

www.codahistory.com

Copyright © 2011 by Coda Books Ltd

All rights reserved. No part of this publication may be reproduced or transmitted in any form or by any means, electronic or mechanical, including photocopy, recording, or any information storage and retrieval system, without permission in writing from the publisher.

A CIP catalogue record for this book is available from the British Library

ISBN: 978-1-908538-92-5

FOREWORD

From 1943 to 1945 the *Waffen SS*, the armed political wing of the *Schutzstaffel* or Nazi party, in the East were engaged in a long and bloody retreat against a numerically far superior enemy. As they fell back across the vast plains of the Soviet Union, Poland, Hungary and ultimately Germany itself, death or ignominious defeat at the hands of the Red Army became their fate. But the *Waffen SS*, true to their character, fought a fanatical rearguard action to the end. In the process they showed utterly heroic if increasingly futile acts of bravery against overwhelming odds.

The turning point in the East was the Soviet Union's vastly superior forces in terms of men, planes and crucially armour which after 1942 began to decisively alter the outcome of the war. While the Germans had developed new tanks such as the Panther and the Tiger to counter the threat of the formidable Soviet T34, they simply could not produce them in sufficient quantities to make a difference. By the end of the war the Germans had produced nearly 6,000 Panthers and just over 1,300 Tiger tanks. In comparison the Russians were building over 1,200 T34 tanks a month.

The devastating defeat at Stalingrad in February 1943 epitomised the changing fortunes of the Germany army or *Wehrmacht* in the East. To counter what he saw as the defeatist attitude of the army, Hitler increasingly turned to the *Waffen SS* whose loyalty and fighting spirit were never in question. The *Wehrmacht's* loss became the *Waffen SS's* gain as the *Führer's* 'fire brigade' were used to plug the gaps and hold the line against the marauding Red Army.

By 1945 under the operational command of Heinrich Himmler Hitler had created 38 *Waffen SS* divisions who had recruited over 900,000 men. As the situation in the East deteriorated they were drawn from an ever more diverse ethnic mix such as the 13th *Waffen SS Handschar* Division which was composed of Bosnian Muslims and conducted anti partisan activities in Yugoslavia and Croatia in 1944. The result was that by the finish of the Second World War nearly half of the *Waffen SS* were non German nationals despite the original strict racial requirements laid down by Himmler.

To the end Hitler possessed an almost blind faith in the fighting ability of the *Waffen SS*. This was despite the fact that many of the later divisions were only regiment or brigade sized units who lacked the experience, élan and cadre of the earlier ones. As losses mounted the original elite existing SS divisions were also amalgamated to form mechanised Panzer Corps which soon became the backbone of the German Army.

In March 1943 Hitler's faith in the SS Panzer Corps was rewarded. Under the charismatic leadership of Paul "Papa" Hauser, nicknamed the father of the *Waffen SS*, they pulled off a spectacular victory at Kharkov, the second largest city in the Ukraine, temporarily halting the Soviet advance. The pictures in this book bear witness to the bravery they showed in the face of an overwhelming enemy.

Hauser's Panzer Corps had found themselves trapped in the city and with the defeat at Stalingrad still a fresh memory Hitler ordered them to "stand fast and fight to the death". Risking Hitlers wrath Hauser ignored him and instead sanctioned a strategic withdraw to prevent his tanks being decimated in the besieged city. In response Hitler flew into a blind rage and tried to sack his wayward commander. However, Hauser regrouped and without Luftwaffe support made a direct attack on Kharkov, eventually recapturing it after four days of intensive, house to house fighting. For his bravery Hauser was awarded the Oak Leaves to his Knights Cross and officially pardoned.

Others honoured with the Knights Cross, the highest award for bravery given by Nazi Germany, included Joachim Peiper who developed a tactic of attacking enemy-held villages by night from all sides while advancing in his armoured half-tracks at full speed, firing at every building. This tactic often set the building's straw roofs on fire and contributed to panic among enemy troops. As a result Peiper's unit gained the nickname the "Blowtorch Battalion".

The Battle of Kharkov was the third time the city had changed sides since the start of Operation Barbarossa or the attack on the Soviet Union began in June 1941. It was also to be the last victory for the *Waffen SS* in the East. The offensive resulted in the Red Army suffering over 70,000 casualties but in an ominous sign of the battles to come the SS Panzer Corps lost nearly half its strength.

Ironically the success of the Third Battle of Kharkov was to prove a turning point in the East not for Hitler but for Stalin because it lulled the Germans back into a false sense of their own superiority. Reinvigorated by the victory, in July 1943 Hitler sought to eliminate the Kursk salient, a bulge where the Soviet advance jutted westwards for about 80 miles into the German line. The result was Operation Citadel, the largest tank battle in history. It pitched 900,000 Germans with 2,700 tanks and 2,000 aircraft against some 1.3 million Russians with 3,600 tanks and 2,400 aircraft. Once again the *Waffen SS* were in the forefront of the fighting.

The German plan was to cut off the Kursk salient by making two pincer attacks at its neck. However, unknown to the Germans the Soviets had received prior intelligence about the attack from the so called 'Lucy' spy ring based in Switzerland, acting on information provided by special operations at Bletchley Park in Oxfordshire. Stalin's commanders had therefore persuaded him to allow the Germans to attack and instead fall back to well prepared defensive positions before counterattacking. The *Waffen SS* fell right into the trap.

On 5 July 1943 the northern offensive was launched and spearheaded by the SS Panzer Corps. Characteristically taking the attack to the enemy, they penetrated deep into the Soviet territory. When the advance eventually slowed after 22 miles of savage fighting, the Germans had destroyed over 1,149 tanks, 459 anti tank guns, 85 aircraft and 47 artillery pieces. However, the Russians fell back on impenetrable defensive positions composed of vast minefields, guns and armour. The Germans offensive stalled and the 1st Soviet Army then counterattacked inflicting large casualties on the SS Panzer Corps, forcing them to retreat. Their fate was sealed a week later when two thousand miles away six US and British divisions landed in Sicily. Fearing an imminent invasion of Italy Hitler diverted the remaining two SS Panzer Corps to the country.

The remains of the *Waffen SS* in the East now found themselves constantly on the retreat. On 25 August Kharkov once again fell to the Soviets, this time for good. By the beginning of September the Germans had suffered over half a million casualties in fifty days and 1,600 tanks and assault guns had been destroyed or knocked out. Soviet casualties are not known but historians estimate them at twice the number of German ones. But for the Hitler the losses were unsustainable and the Battle of Kursk proved to be the last German offensive in the East. Alexander Kovalenko, a Soviet pilot, flying over a battlefield littered with German armour declared triumphantly "The enemy's front is broken. We are advancing".

After Kursk morale in the army began to disintegrate but in the

Waffen SS a fanatical, if increasingly futile, fighting spirit lived on. Panzer officer Tassilo von Bogenhardt was typical and said after the battle "Each German soldier considered himself superior to any single Russian, even though their numbers were so overpowering. The slow, orderly retreat did not depress us too much. We felt we were holding our own". His illusion was rudely shattered shortly afterwards when he was badly wounded and then captured by the Soviets, the worst fate that could befall a *Waffen SS* soldier.

By the end of 1943 half the territory taken by the Germans since 1941 was back under Soviet control. Russia had lost over twenty million men or nearly eighty per cent of its total war casualties. But they were no longer on their own. The Allies had successfully invaded Italy and six months later on 6 June 1944 came the D-Day landings. For the *Waffen SS* this meant fighting on two fronts and more divisions being diverted from the East to the West, further weakening their ability to defend the 'Fatherland against Bolshevism'.

Even in retreat, however, the *Waffen SS* proved themselves to be a formidable fighting unit. Typical was Herbert Gille, commander of the 5.SS-Panzer Division *"Wiking"* and pictured in his book. In an almost suicidal move he broke out of the Korsun-Cherkassy Pocket in Northern Ukraine in 1944 against overwhelming Russian odds. For his bravery he received the Diamonds to add to his Knight Cross. Also pictured is *Obertsturmbannführer* or Lietenant Colonel Leon Degrelle, commander of the 28th *Waffen SS* Division *"Walloon"* from Belgium. During the retreat of his division to the border of Germany in 1944 he was severely wounded but carried on fighting. As a result he was one of only three foreigners to win the Oak Leaves to the Knights Cross. He received it from Hitler's hands and later claimed Hitler told him "if I had a son, I wish he'd resemble you".

On May day 1944 Stalin declared "If we are to deliver our country and those of our allies from the danger of enslavement, we must pursue the wounded German beast and deliver the final blow to him in his own lair". The Soviets started their pursuit on 22 June 1944 when they launched Operation Bagration, the largest and last offensive to be launched from Russian soil. This left the remaining *Waffen SS* divisions defending a 1,000 mile front with few reserves. It was the beginning of the end.

As the war in the East moved to Poland and eventually Germany, *Waffen SS* troops were among the final soldiers defending the ruins of the Reich Chancellery in Berlin as Hitler committed suicide on 30 April 1945. When news of his death reached them, many of the remaining *Waffen SS* troops shot themselves rather than surrender to the Soviets.

After hostilities had finally ceased on 8 May 1945 nearly one in three *Waffen SS* troops were dead or missing in action. For an elite fighting force which never made up more than 10% of the total German Army and had numbered just 133 men in 1933, they had fought with almost reckless courage and paid a very high price. Their mortality rate was the equivalent of all the casualties suffered by the United States military during the entire war.

The *Waffen SS* had been overwhelmed by an enemy simply too strong in men and material. However, as their military situation had worsened so had their atrocities while some non combat units were directly culpable when it came to the Holocaust. Praise for them as an elite fighting force in the annals of the Second World War therefore needs to be balanced against the utter ruthlessness they showed, particularly towards the Jews, Soviets and later the Poles in the putting down of the Warsaw uprising in 1944. Accordingly history has judged them not as they would have wished by their combat record but instead far more ignominiously by the atrocities they carried out.

War crimes aside, the military esteem the *Waffen SS* were held in can perhaps best be judged not by their rivals in the *Wehrmacht* but by their hated adversaries in the Red Army. At the victory parade in Red Square in Moscow on 24 June 1945, pride of place among the captured Nazi standards went to the First *Waffen SS* division, the *Leibstandarte Adolf Hitler*.

The Third Battle of Kharkov was last major victory in the East for the *Waffen SS*. Sepp Dietrich, commander of the *Leibstandarte Adolf Hitler*, presenting the Knights Cross medal to, from left, Max Hansen, Hans Becker and Hermann Weiser. Part of the Panzer Corps under Paul Hauser, they played a key role in the battle against far superior Soviet forces.

Commanders of the *Leibstrandarte Adolf Hitler* line up for a group photograph following the success of the Third Battle of Kharkov. 1st row: Ewert Staudinger, Besuden, Kurt "Panzer" Meyer, Sepp Dietrich, Weiser, Sandig, Bludau and Schonberger. 2nd and 3rd row: Siebken, Becker, Wisch, Westernflagen, Kraas, Gunther, Lehmann, Frey, Hubert Meyer, Maab, Krause.

The Third Battle of Kharkov resulted in many Knights Crosses being awarded in April 1943 From left to right - Sylvester Stadler, Hans Weiß, Christian Tychsen, Otto Kumm, Vinzenz Kaiser and Karl-Heinz Worthmann.

In Russia during the summer of 1943 German optimism quickly gave way to increasing pessimism after the Battle of Kursk. From left to right the *Führer der Waffen SS*, *Obergruppenführer* (Colonel General) Walter Krüger (with Knight's Cross), *Obersturmbannführer* (Lieutenant General) Hans-Albin von Reitzenstein, Paul Hasser, and *Oberführer* (Senior Colonel) Werner Ostendorff.

Paul Hauser in conversation with Kurt "Panzer" Meyer. He captured the Red Square in Kharkov and defended it against vastly superior forces. Meyer was later to become one of the youngest divisional commanders in the German Army.

Senior Officers from the Panzer Corps discuss tactics over a bottle of wine in the mess. From the left: Hauser, Dietrich, Gille and Panzer "Meyer".

Officers from the Panzer Corps prepare for the next offensive. From the left: Prieß, Gille, Kruger, and Dietrich.

Tiger tanks advance in Operation Citadel or the Battle of Kursk. Although superior in fire power and armour to the Soviet T34, the Germans had too few of them.

Inside a Tiger tank: the driver (above), and the radio operator (right).
 When introduced in August 1942 it was the most powerful tank in the world and continued to cause both military and psychological fear in the Soviets until the end of the war. Its highly accurate gun would allow the crew to engage and destroy enemy tanks up to 2,000 meters away.

Inside a Tiger tank: The gunner (above), and the commander (right).

With its 88mm gun the Tiger was feared by the Soviets but was over engineered, expensive to produce and difficult to repair. As a result only 1,300 were made during the whole war.

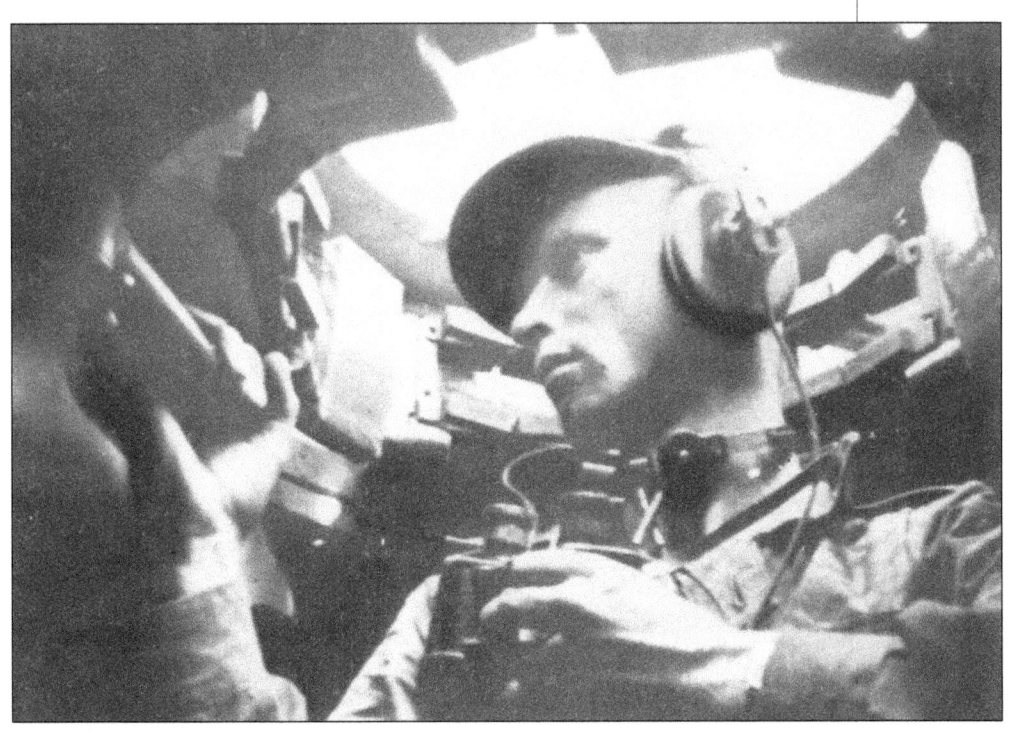

Panzers are massed for a concentrated attack during "Operation Citadel".

Panther tanks, half tracks and Panzer III tanks assemble ready prior to the start of the battle. The Panzer III was the mainstay of the German forces but was completely outclassed by the Soviet T34.

Waffen SS troops with their distinctive camouflage uniforms assess enemy positions, July 1943

A half track with a 75mm PaK anti tank gun. The weapon was effective against nearly every Allied tank until the end of the war.

A Tiger tank ready for action. Developed in 1942 the official German designation was *Panzerkampfwagen* Tiger Ausf. E, often shortened to Tiger.

Soldiers advance in a *Waffen SS Sonderkraftfahrzeug* 251 or Sd.Kfz251 halftrack. It was the largest and best armoured German halftrack and was designed to take the *Panzergrenadiers* or the motorised infantry into battle.

Troops from the SS *Das Reich* Division advance as a Tiger follows. The Battle of Kursk pitched 900,000 Germans with 2,700 tanks and 2,000 aircraft against some 1.3 million Russians with 3,600 tanks and 2,400 aircraft.

Members of the *Waffen SS* discuss tactics with a tank commander and then move into position. Operation Citadel was the largest tank battle in history.

Captain Hans Becker, SS *Hauptsturmführer* was awarded the Knight's Cross on 23 March 1943 following the Third Battle of Kharkov. He commanded the 2nd Company, of the 2nd SS Panzer Grenadier Regiment, *Leibstandarte Adolf Hitler*. Becker was killed a year and a half later in France.

Waffen SS infantrymen advance carrying boxes of ammunition. The Kursk salient was a trap because the Soviets had got prior warning about the German offensive from the 'Lucy' spy ring in Switzerland.

Operation Citadel begins. The German plan was to cut off the Kursk salient by making two pincer attacks at its neck.

Infantrymen mark the forward edge of the battleline for the combat aircraft.

Engineers sweep and mark mine fields.

The Soviets retreated behind five defensive positions riddled with tens of thousands of mines before counterattacking.

In the opening days of the Battle of Kursk the *Waffen SS* made rapid progress penetrating deep into Soviet territory.

A command post in a Russian tank trench.

Russian resistance stiffens. SS-units are confronted with elite Soviet troops while Ju 87 Stuka dive-bombers try to open a passage through enemy lines.

Sturmbannführer (Major) Joachim Peiper with his adjutant Werner Wolff in the command post. Peiper was awarded the Knights Cross for bravery in the Battle of Kharkov in March 1943. He developed a tactic of attacking enemy-held villages by night from all sides while advancing in his armoured half-tracks at full speed, firing at every building. This tactic often set the building's straw roofs on fire and contributed to panic among enemy troops. As a result Peiper's unit gained the nickname the "Blowtorch Battalion".

Destroyed Russian T-34 tank. Due to its sloping armour and firepower it was to prove a formidable opponent. However, during the first few days of the offensive the momentum was with the Germans and many T34 tanks were knocked out by Tiger, Panthers and *Jadpanzers* IV Sd.Kfz.or tank destroyers.

Armoured infantrymen shelter behind a destroyed T34 tank.

The German offensive soon ran into trouble when the Soviets retreated behind defensive lines which had been prepared weeks earlier.

A portrait of Staff Sergeant or *Oberscharführer* Kurt Sametreiter after he had just received the Knights Cross. In the tank Battle of Prokhorovka, part of the Battle of Kursk, he was a platoon commander in the 3rd Company, 1st *Panzerjäger* Battalion of the 1st SS Division *Leibstandarte SS Adolf Hitler*. *Leibstandarte* was then part of the 2nd SS Panzer Corps and was attacked by two Russian Tank Corps. He received the medal for destroying twenty four tanks in one action.

As the Germans pushed forward the Soviets waited for their chance to counterattack. The faces of these young *Waffen SS* infantrymen already show the exhaustion of battle.

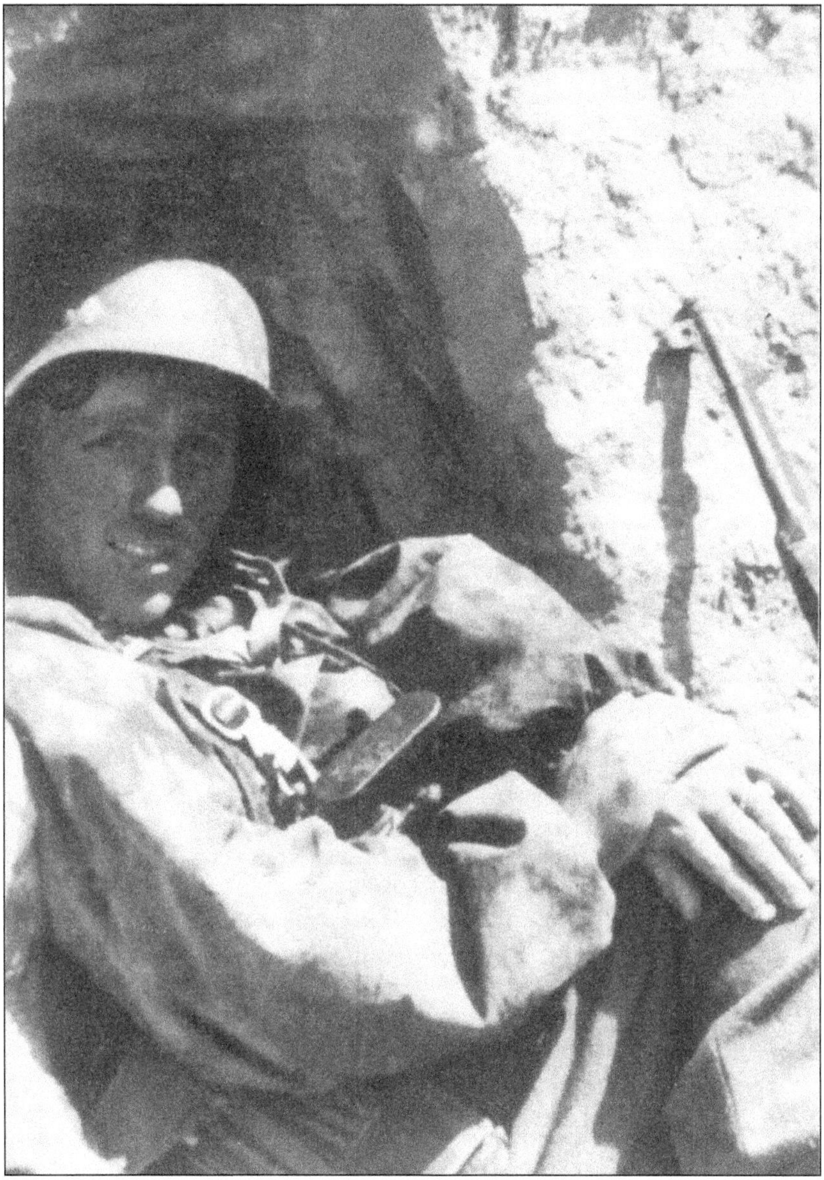

As the Germans continued the advance they had no idea that the battle plans to eliminate the Kursk bulge had been leaked to Stalin. Despite mounting losses the Germans continued to push forward, falling ever deeper into the Soviets trap.

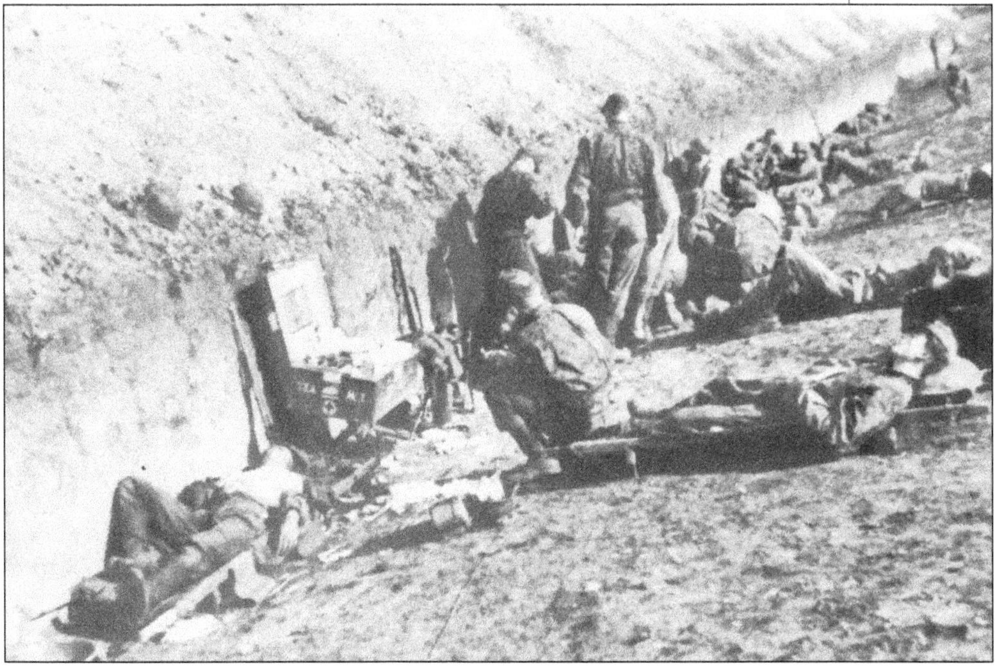

Colonel or *Standartenführer* Heinz Harmel, commander of the SS Infantry Regiment "*Deutschland*" scans the horizon from his command vehicle and relaxes in a dug out. He distinguished himself by attacking with his regiment at night. For his bravery in the Battle of Kursk he received on September 7 1943 the Oak Leaves to go with his Knights Cross.

Harmel drinks a toast to two of his men, G.E Wisliceny and Helmut Schreiber who have just received the Knights Cross.

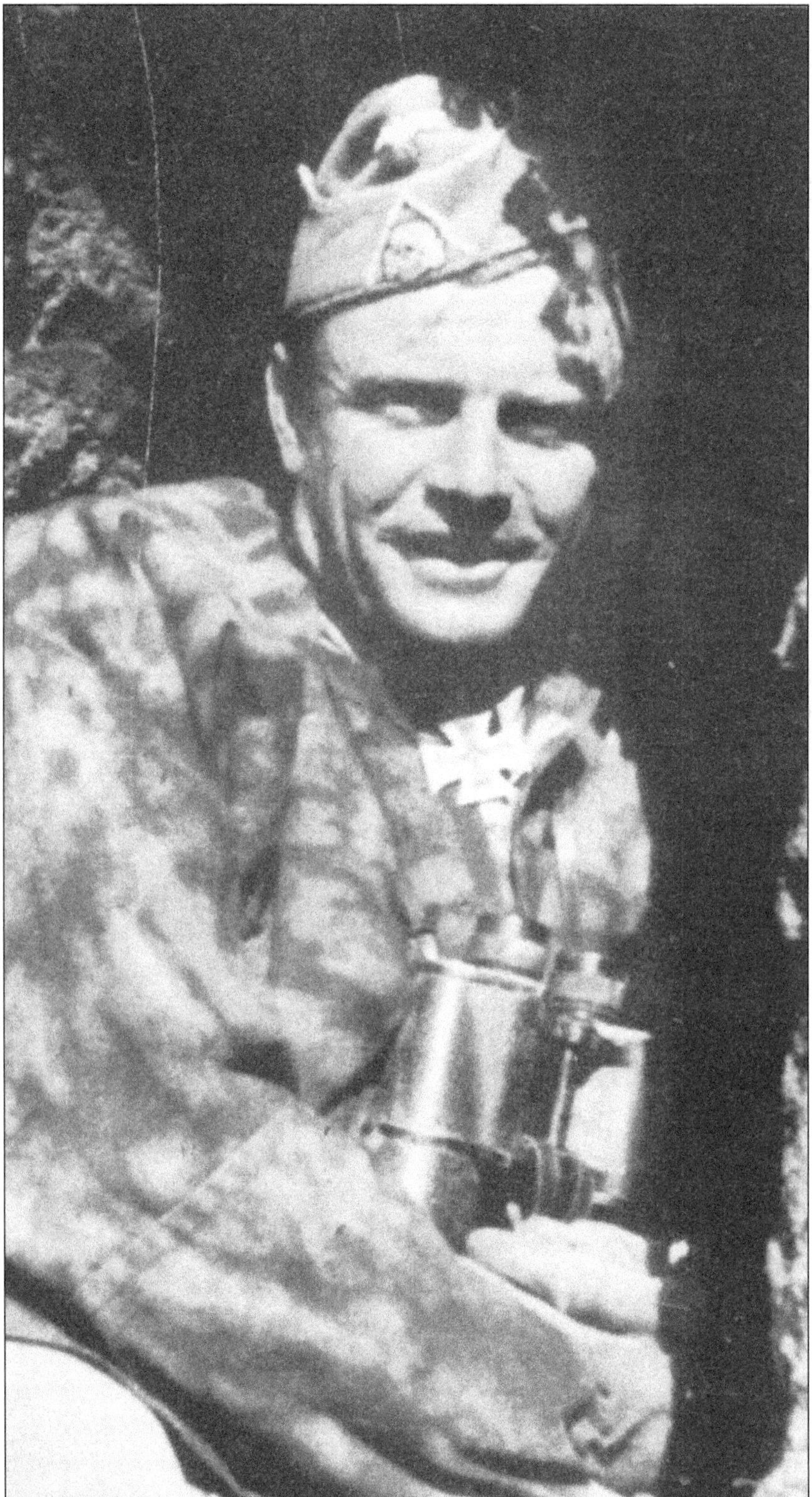

Germans retreat under heavy fire. Within a few days of the attack the offensive ground to halt after 22 miles. The Soviets who had fallen back on vast minefields, guns and armour then counter attacked with their tanks

The charred remains of trees bear testimony to the intensity of the battle.

Waffen SS troops retreat across a river. The Soviets made full use of the natural features around Kursk to pursue and attack the Germans knowing they were vulnerable crossing water.

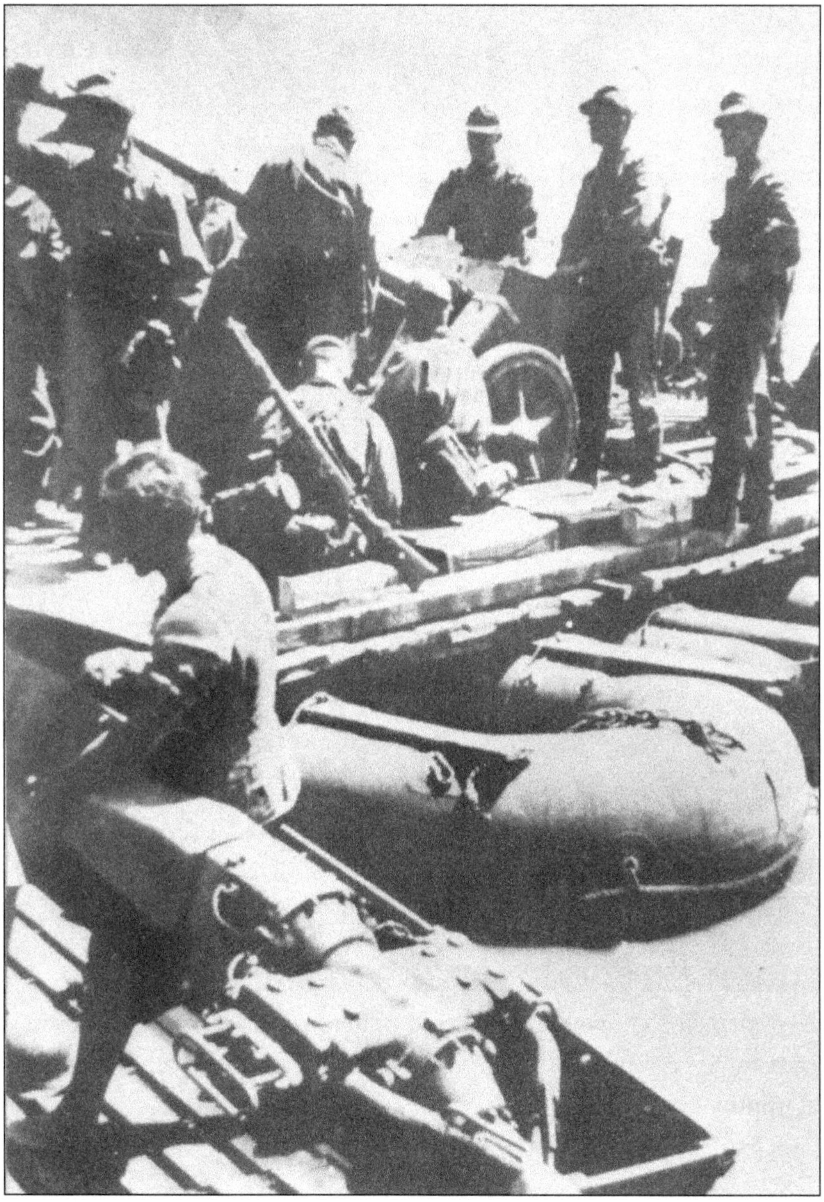

A *Waffen* SS commander on a horse watches as his men gingerly cross a river on a very make shift bridge. *Waffen* SS engineers became very good at improvising.

Waffen SS troops take cover in a ditch. Defeat is etched on their faces.

The retreat was slowed by the poor conditions of the Russian roads which even in summer could become impassable after a flash storm.

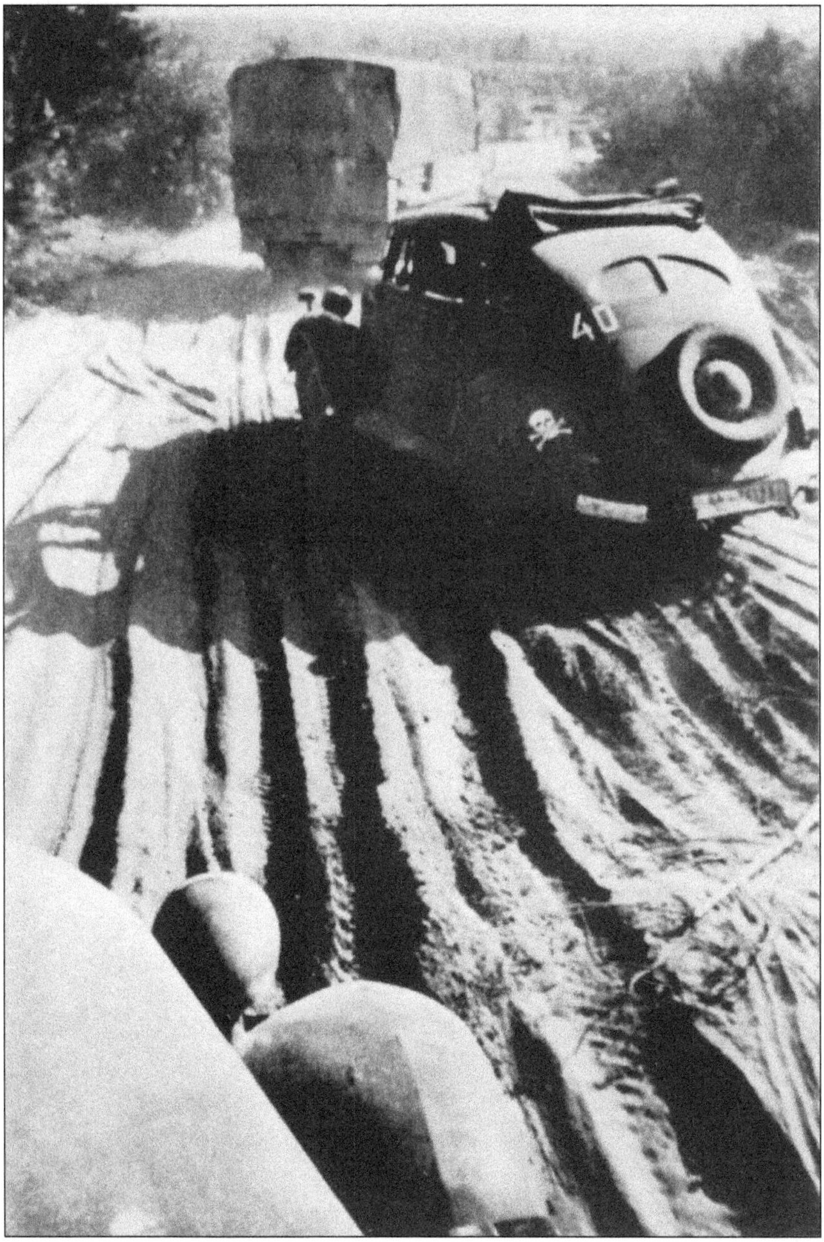
40

Waffen SS soldiers received better rations than *Wehrmacht* troops reflecting their elite status in the eyes of Hitler and Himmler. It often caused resentment among regular troops.

Food was essential to maintain the morale of the troops.

This even extended to real luxuries like champagne.

After the Battle of Kursk was lost, the Germans were effectively in retreat for the rest of the war in the East. *Waffen SS* troops were used strategically to slow the Russian advance and impose the maximum number of casualties on the advancing Soviets. In this way it was hoped that they would sue for peace.

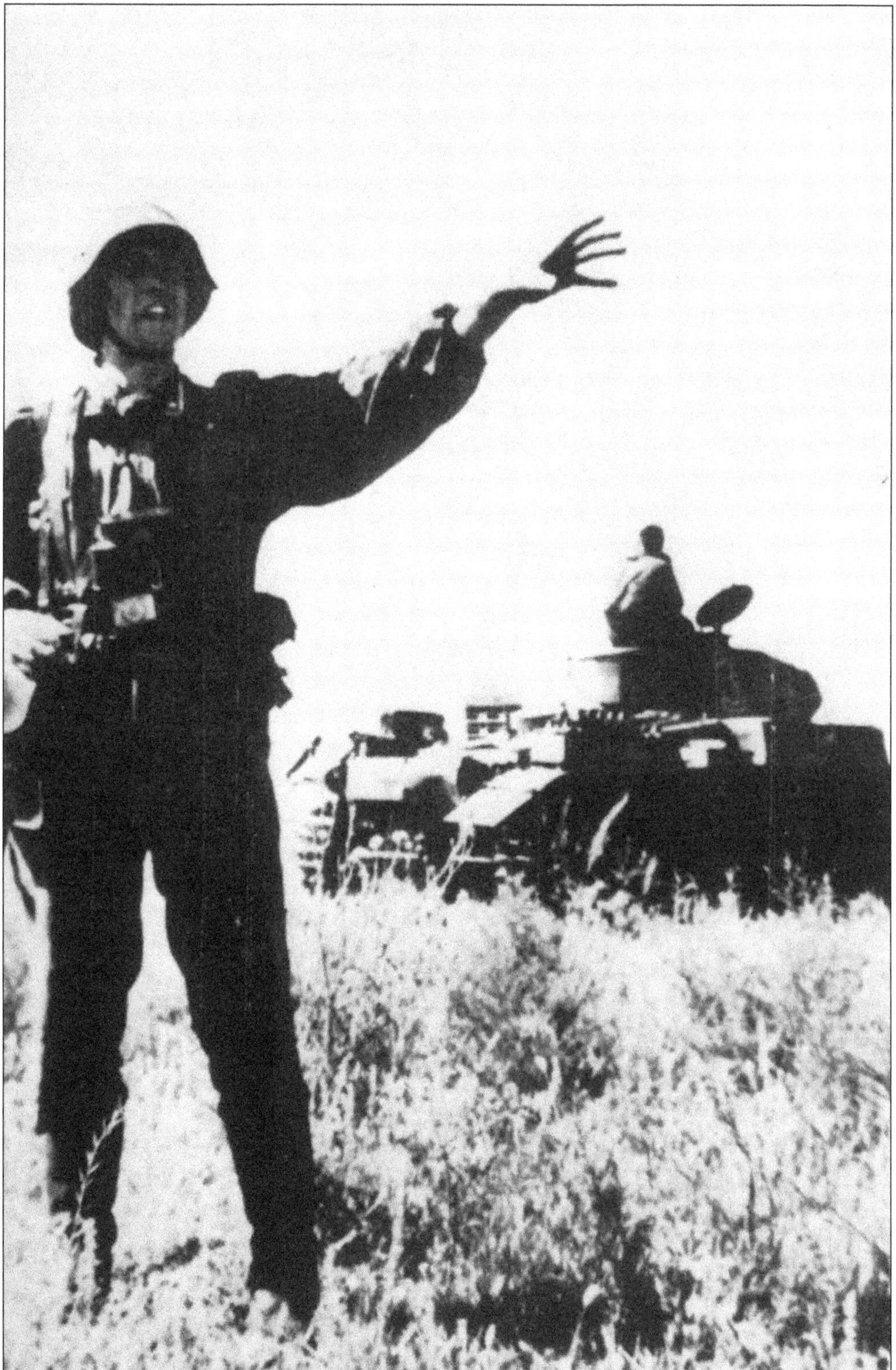

A *Waffen SS* Grenadier with a Mauser K98 rifle contemplates the fate of his unit.

Waffen SS troops capture a child partisan in August 1943. The Soviets made widespread use of children for guerrilla activities.

During the long retreat *Waffen SS* units would often counterattack the advancing Russians, giving the regular army time to withdraw to more strategic lines of defence. However, they only brought temporary relief due to the sheer weight of numbers the Soviets were throwing into the advance.

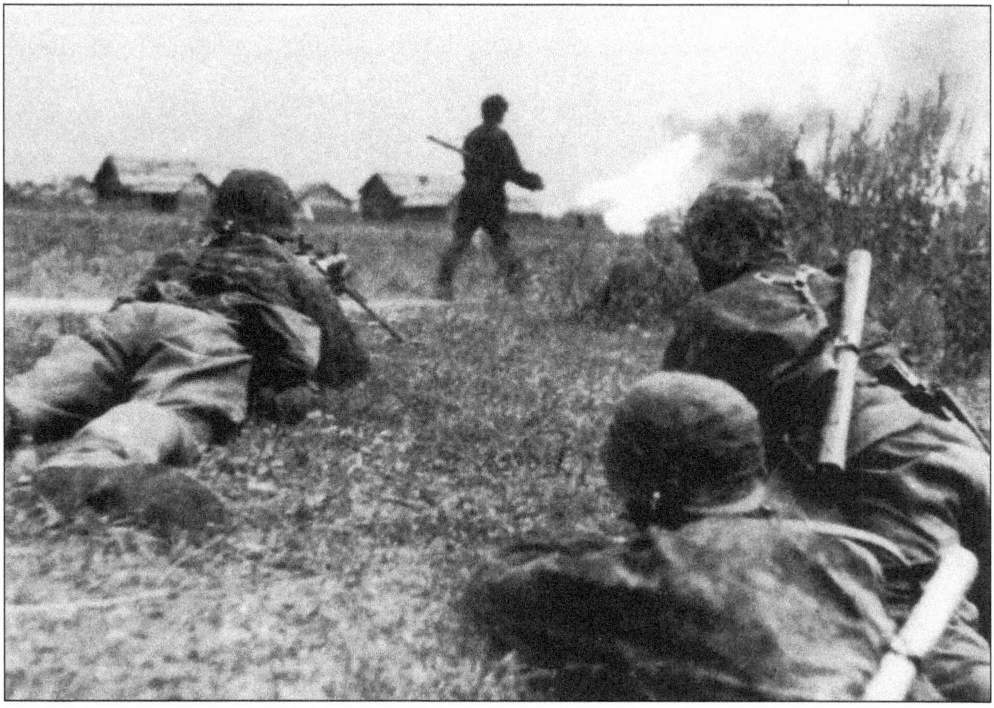

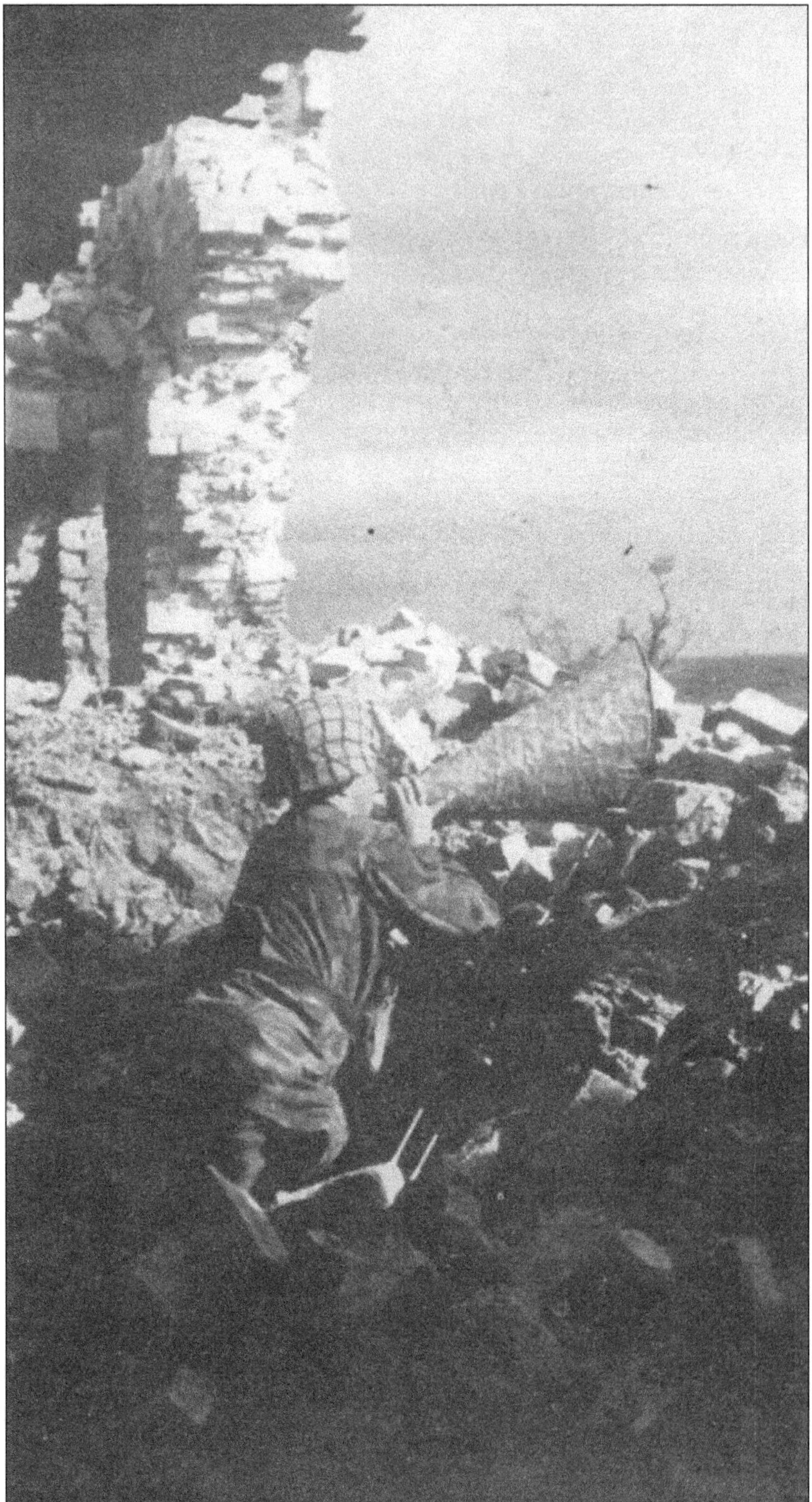

German troops in the rubble of Stalingrad use a megaphone to surrender while others use a scissor periscope to assess their situation. By February 1943 the German 6th Army had either surrendered or been destroyed.

As the Germans retreated they found themselves at the mercy of not just the Soviet army but also of the Russian landscape. Some of the most bitter fighting took place in the great swamps and forests of northern Russia and the Baltic States.

Supplying the troops with ammunition became a major logistical challenge in these areas.

Waffen SS troops under fire in the Battle of Narva in 1944. Joined by Estonian volunteers the *Waffen SS* fought a very successful rearguard action depriving Stalin of Estonia as a base for air and seaborne attacks against Finland for seven and a half months.

Adolf Peichl, a second lieutenant in *Das Reich*, awards one of his men with a gold tank destruction badge for destroying five tanks. Peichel himself destroyed 11 tanks.

The grave of an ethnic German Gerhard Harder who was forcefully conscripted into the Soviet Army. After he was taken prisoner by the Germans he served with the *Waffen SS*.

A *Waffen SS* recruiting poster for the French or Charlemagne Division. Realising what would happen to them when Germany lost, they fought fanatically and were among the troops defending the Reich Chancellery in April 1945.

Recruiting poster for the 20th Grenadier SS Division, the 1st Estonian. Compulsory conscription was introduced on 20 January 1944 by the German authorities.

A signpost just outside Leningrad showing it was over 2611 km to Oslo. The German retreat in the East would stretch to over 800 miles ending in the catacomb of Berlin.

Dutch, Norwegian and Finnish volunteers in the *Waffen SS*.

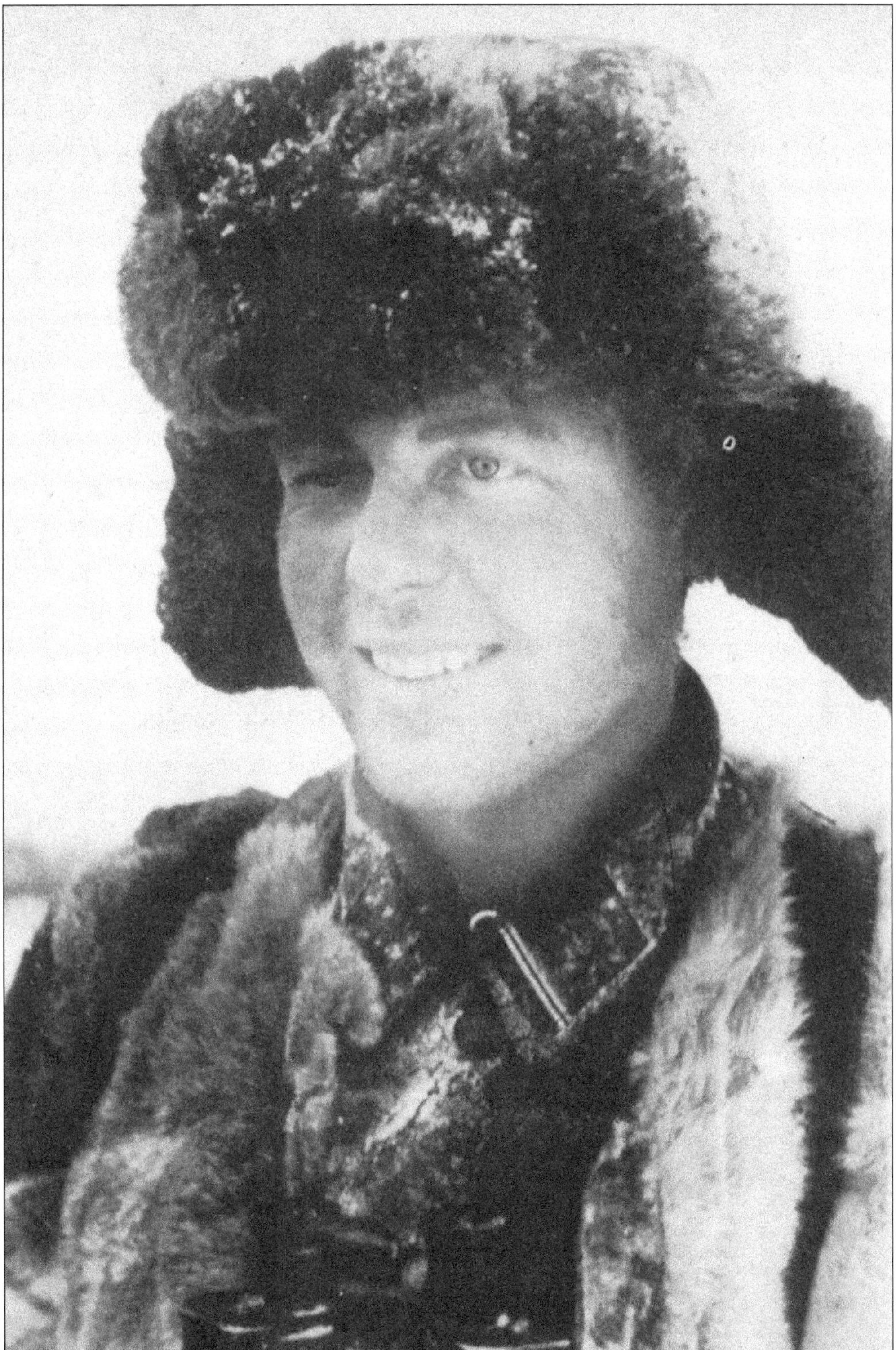

Women were also recruited for medical and other support roles. By 1945 nearly half of *Waffen SS* were non German nationals despite the original strict racial requirements laid down by Heinrich Himmler.

Flag of the Danish *Frikorps* or Free Corps. Formed in 1941 on the eve of Operation Barbarossa nearly 10,000 Danes, mostly of German ethnic origin, volunteered. It was disbanded in 1943.

The grave of a Danish *Frikorps* commander *Obsturmbannführer* Lieutenant Colonel Graf von Schalburg.

The SS Division "*Nord*" was is involved in heavy defensive fighting in Finland.

The Finnish General Lauri Malmberg, commander of the Finnish Civil Guard, together with the *Waffen SS* division commander Matthias Kleinheisterkamp who was posthumously awarded the Oak Leaves to go with his Knights Cross.

German troops head out on horse back through the cold Finnish winter of 1944. The Finns surrendered on 4 September 1944 and an armistice was signed with Moscow on 19 September 1944.

A German self propelled assault gun. They inflicted large losses on the retreating Russians but in the end sheer weight of number overwhelmed them. As the Soviets retreated they saw at first hand what the Germans had employed a scorched earth policy in their towns and villages which simply hardened their resolve.

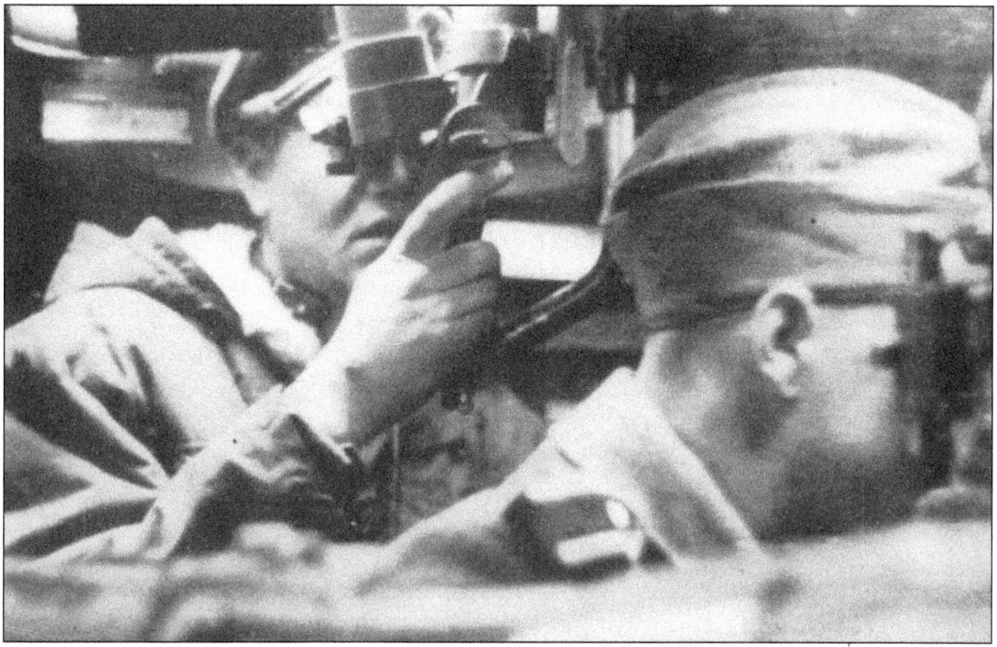

A German PaK 40 75mm anti tank gun. This was the backbone of German anti tank guns in the final years of the war.

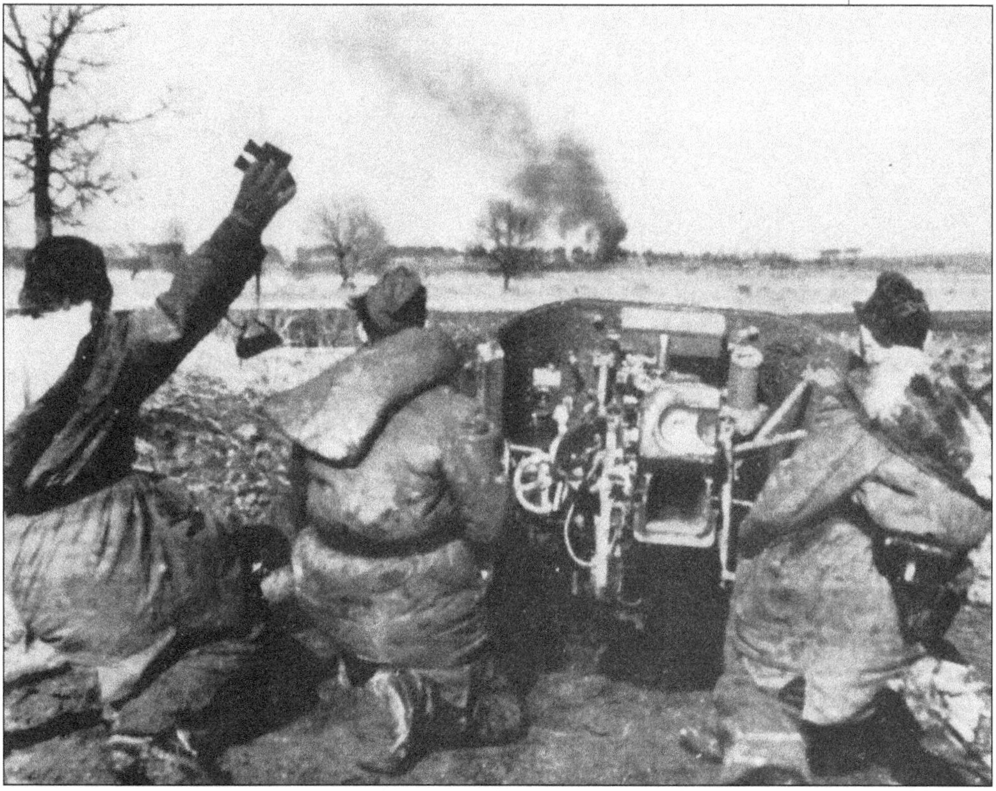

The Tiger tank was far superior to the Soviet T34. But there simply wasn't enough of them. By the end of the war the Germans had produced nearly 6,000 Panthers and just over 1,300 Tiger tanks. In comparison the Russians were building over 1,200 T34 tanks a month.

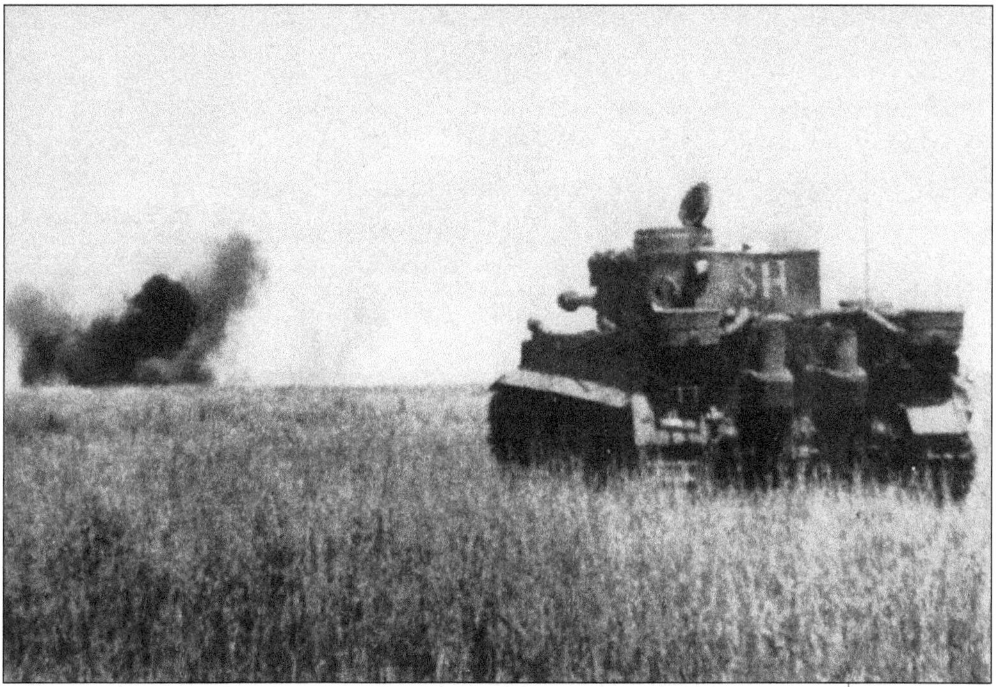
SH

Waffen SS soldiers watch the German retreat. Despite morale plummeting in the *Wehrmacht*, the *Waffen SS* maintained a fanatical fighting spirit to the end.

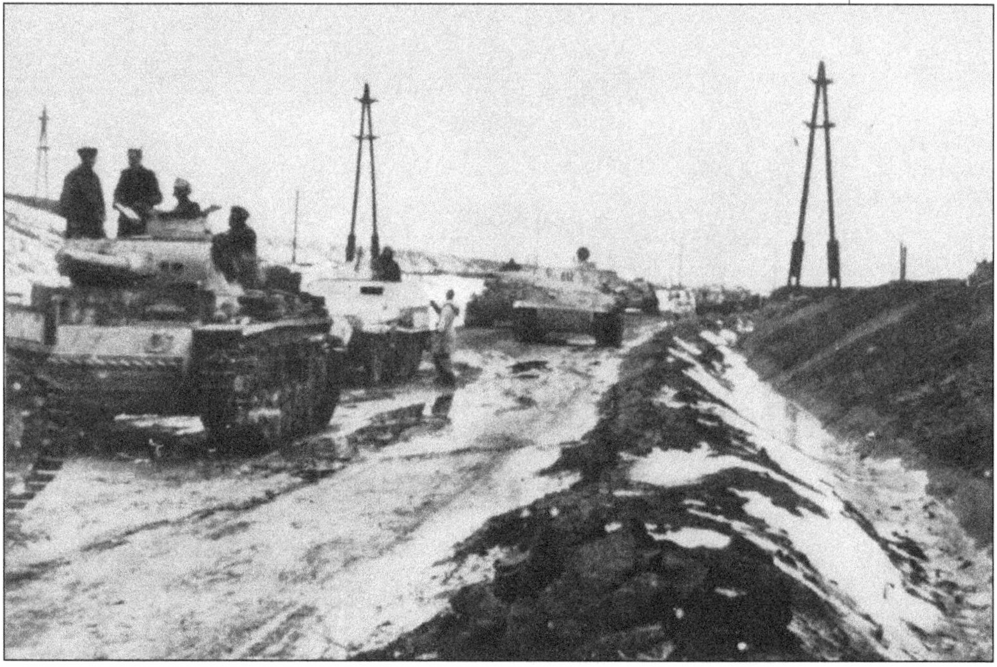

The third winter of fighting in Russia was particularly hard because the Germans were in full retreat. Hitler's orders to "stand fast and fight to the death" resulted in the needless death of many *Waffen SS* troops.

Tiger tanks retreat through the Russian winter in December 1943. Its formidable 88m gun was feared by the Soviets but it over enginerred and consequently proved difficult to repair.

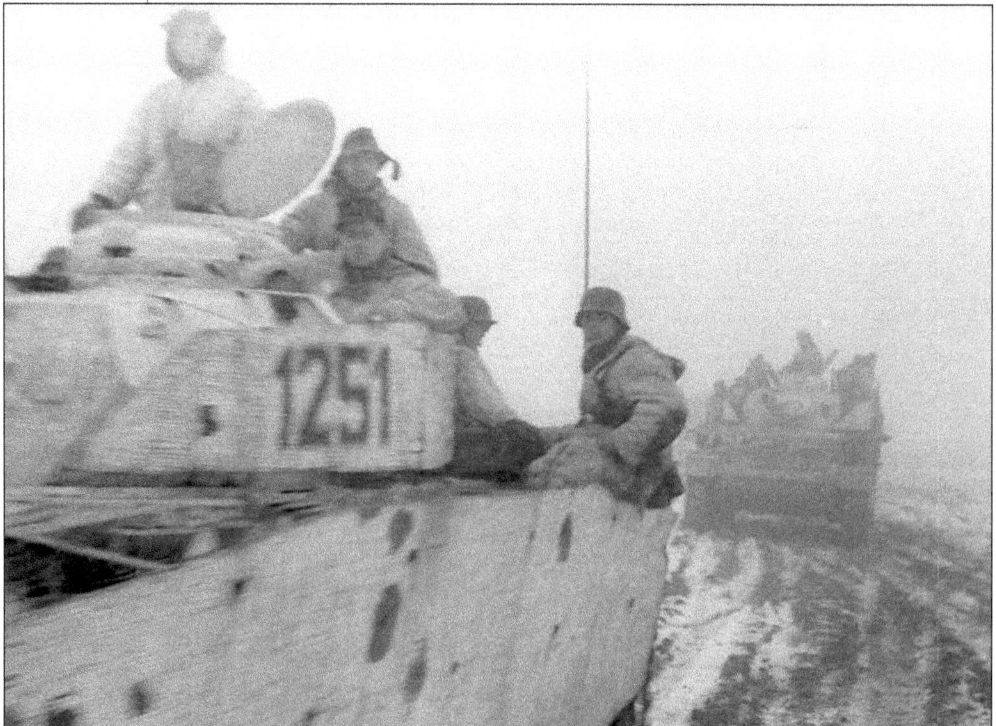
1251

A German soldier up to his waist in snow makes slow progress with his MG42 machine gun. The weather compounded the Germans' misery.

The 5th Waffen SS Division *Wiking* led a brave break out from the Kowel or Kovel pocket in 1944. Utterly heroic if increasingly futile acts of bravery against overwhelming odds were a speciality of the *Waffen SS*.

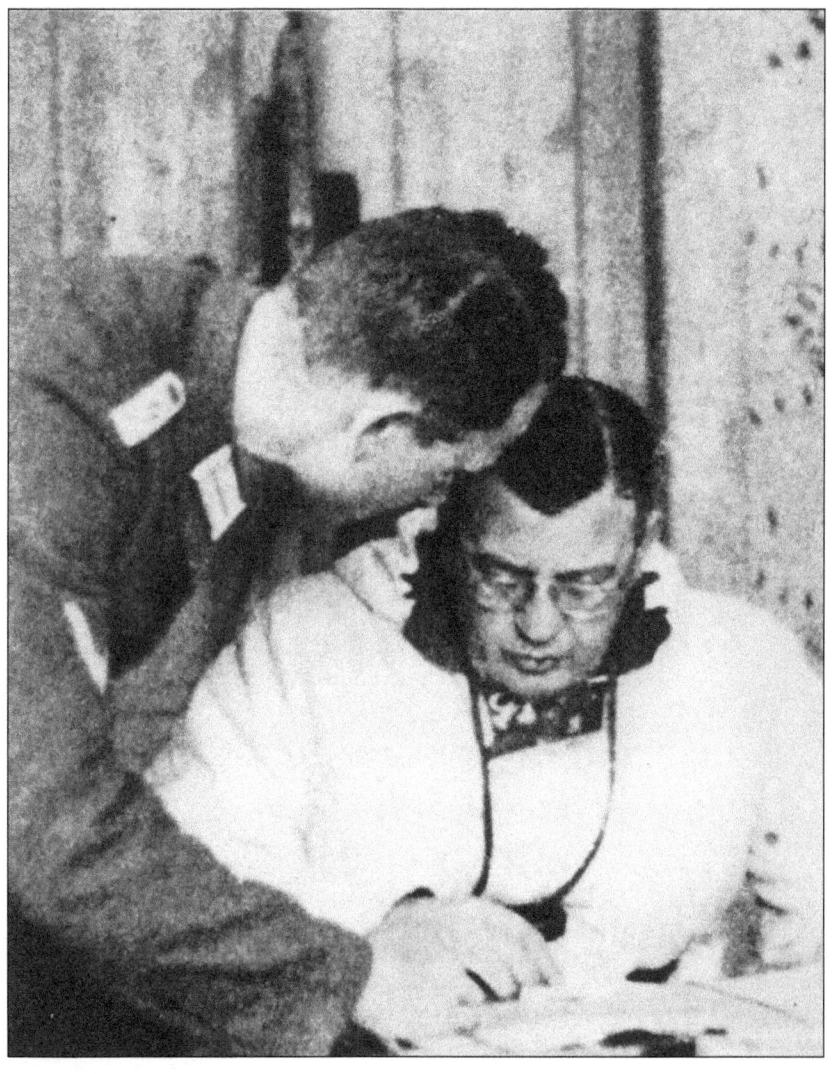

SS-Lieutenant Colonel *Gruppenführer* Eich von dem Bach who led the breakout.

Soviet propaganda leaflet asks the Germans whether they want life or death.

Supplies are dropped to encircled German troops in the East. From 1944 onwards the *Luftwaffe* was rarely seen along the Eastern Front.

Herbert Gille, commander of the 5.SS-Panzer Division "*Wiking*".

Gille won the Knight's Cross, 1944. In an almost suicidally brave move he received the Diamonds to his Knight Cross for breaking out of the Korsun-Cherkassy or Tscherkassy Pocket in Northen Ukraine against overwhelming Russian odds and ended the war as the most highly decorated *Waffen SS* commander.

Colonel or *Standartenführer* Wilhelm Trabandt (second, front row) visits the 1 SS Infantry Brigade. It was a unit formed from former concentration camp guards who took part in anti partisan activities and the extermination of the Jews. In 1944 the Brigade was used as the cadre in the formation of the 18th SS Volunteer Panzergrenadier Division Horst Wessel.

Erich von dem Bach-Zelewski attends briefing, March 1944. He later in August 1944 went on to ruthlessly put down the Warsaw uprising.

A *Waffen SS Totenkopf* soldier and *Wehrmacht* infantry troops discuss tactics in front of a destroyed Russian T34 tank.

Members of the 13th *Waffen SS* Handschar Division which was composed of Bosnia Muslims. It was a mountain infantry division that conducted anti partisan activities in Yugoslavia and Croatia in 1944.

13th *Waffen SS* Handschar Division troops scale a cliff, May 1944.

Waffen SS with wreaths for Colonel Voldemars Veiss funeral, April 1944. He was a Colonel in the Latvian army and a prominent Nazi sympathiser.

The break-outs from the Kowel and Korsun-Cherkassy or Tscherkassy pockets against overwhelming Soviet odds sealed the fanatical fighting spirit of the *Waffen SS "Wiking"* Division.

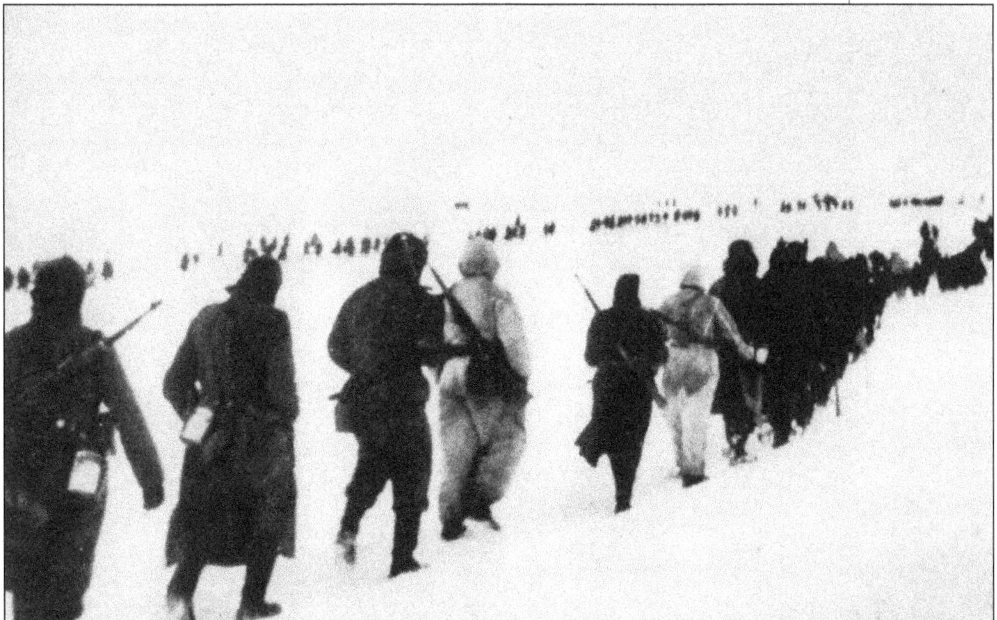

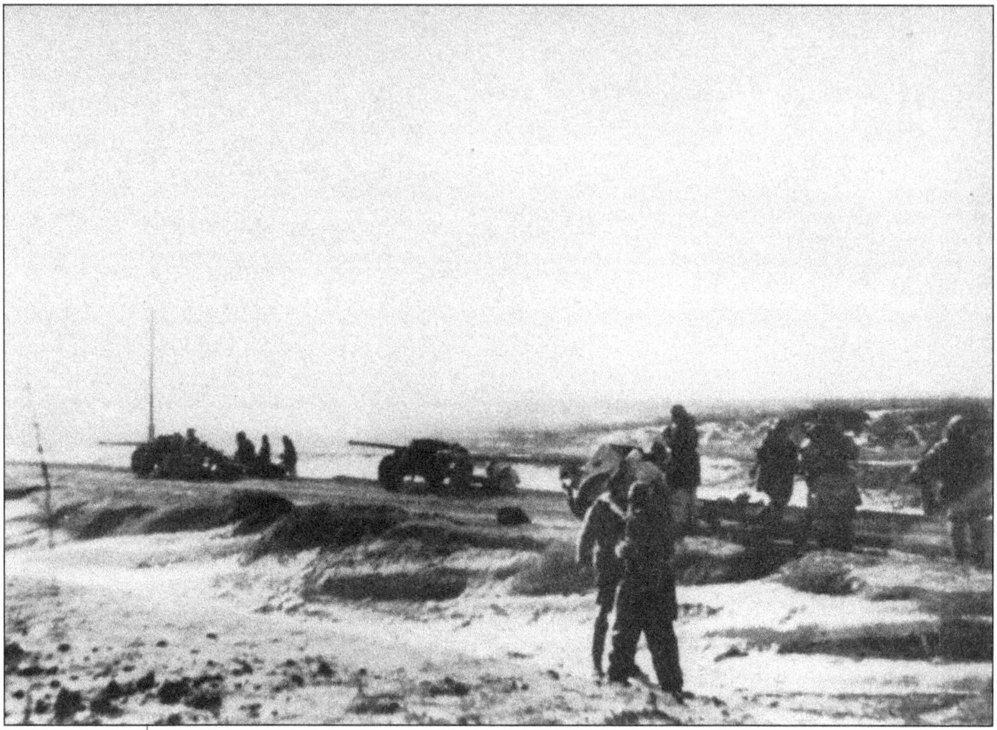

Anti-tank guns and self-propelled field guns protect the flanks during the break-out.

Panther tanks of the "*Wiking*" tank regiment played a decisive part in the successful break out from the Korsun-Tscherkassy Pocket. It easily outclassed any Soviet tank and was meant to replace the Panzer III and IVs which were susceptible to the Soviet T34 but was never made in enough numbers.

A break between operations. On the left: The commander of a Panther tank unit reports to *Gruppenführer* or Lieutenant Colonel Gille. On the right: The commander of the tank regiment: Johannes-Rudolf Mühlenkamp.

SS *Obersturmführer* or Lieutenant Colonel Erwin Meier-Dress, Knights Cross, August 1944. A Panzer Ace, he was killed a year later trying to relieve the Soviet siege of Budapest.

Panther tanks of the SS Division *"Wiking"* fighting east of Warsaw.

Waffen SS troops are sent in to put down the Warsaw uprising, August 1944. They did but with characteristic ruthlessness.

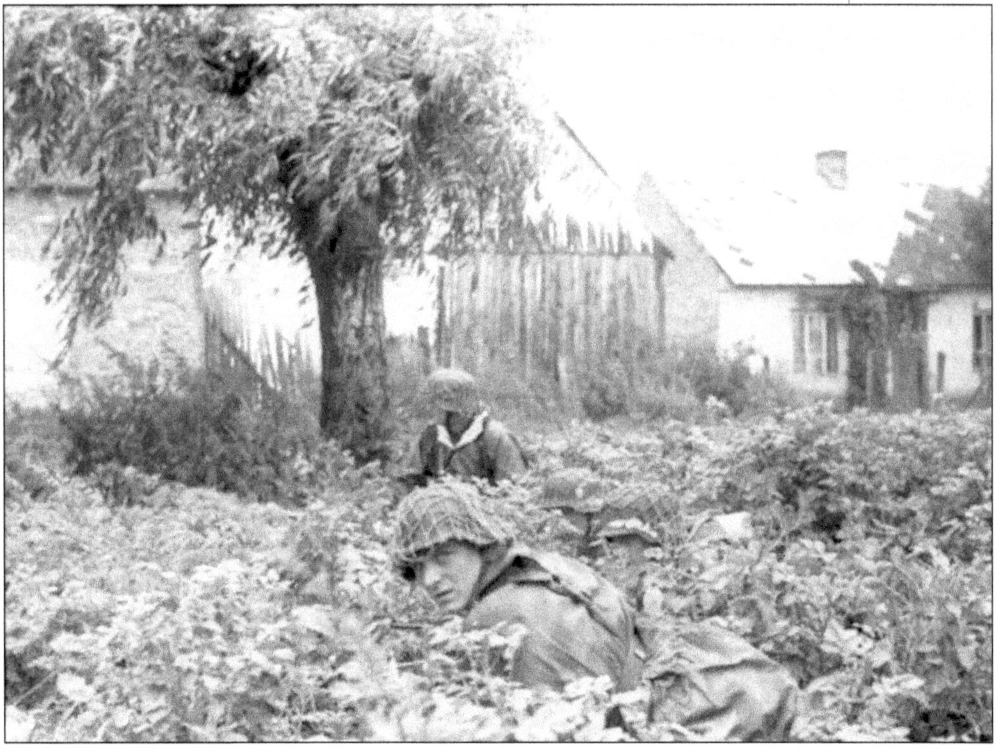

Civilians flee the fighting.

Waffen SS troops round up members of the Polish resistance Home Army.

Exhausted *Waffen SS* troops push supplies up to the front in an improvised cart attached to a bicycle. Controversially the Soviets stopped short of the city allowing the Germans to put down the uprising. The Poles held out for 63 days with little outside support.

German troops rest during the uprising. 16,000 Poles died, German casualties were about 8,000. But the real victims were the civilians of Warsaw. Between 150,000 and 200,000 of them died, mostly from the fighting and mass murder.

Waffen SS troops pose for the camera. German propaganda successfully expolited the futility of the Warsaw uprising up as a salutary lesson to others.

Initially the Poles took over the city centre but in savage house to house fighting the Germans took back control in September 1944. In all 25% of Warsaw buildings were destroyed and together with earlier damage over 85% of the city had been razed to the ground when the Soviets finally entered in January 1945.

A cemetery of the SS Division "*Wiking*" in Uspenskaja, Russia.

All the headstones have been removed to prevent them being desecrated by the Red Army.

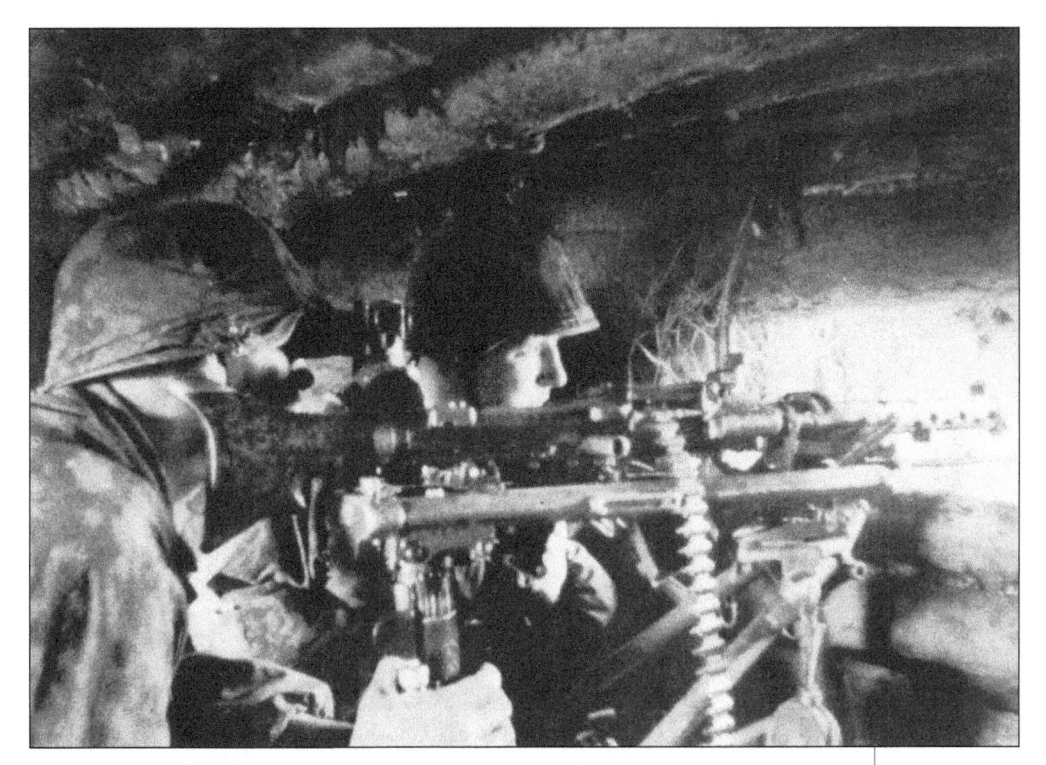

The cost in lives of defending the constantly German line against the vast numerical superiority of the Russian forces always fell disproportionately on infantrymen.

Waffen SS troops under fire. Feared and loathed by the Soviets in equal measure, if they were captured they were often executed on sight.

A shell explodes just in front of a unit of *Waffen SS* troops. During the long retreat in the East they were used strategically, often to relive encircled *Wehrmacht* divisions.

The Russians enter a village in Poland as *Waffen SS* troops seek to counterattack. Even their bravery could not make up for the Soviets overwhelming superiority in men and material.

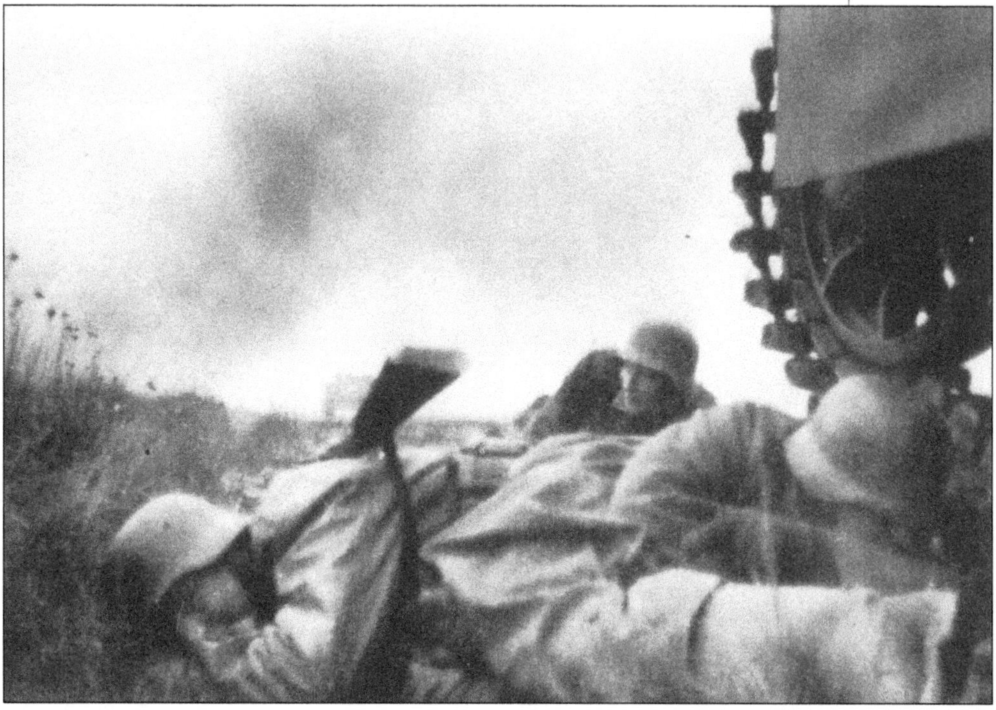

Detroyed Soviet T34 tanks litter a battlefield as *Waffen SS* troops look on. The Russians paid a huge price in liberating their homeland and fighting their way to the centre of Berlin, with over 20 million dead, both civilian and military.

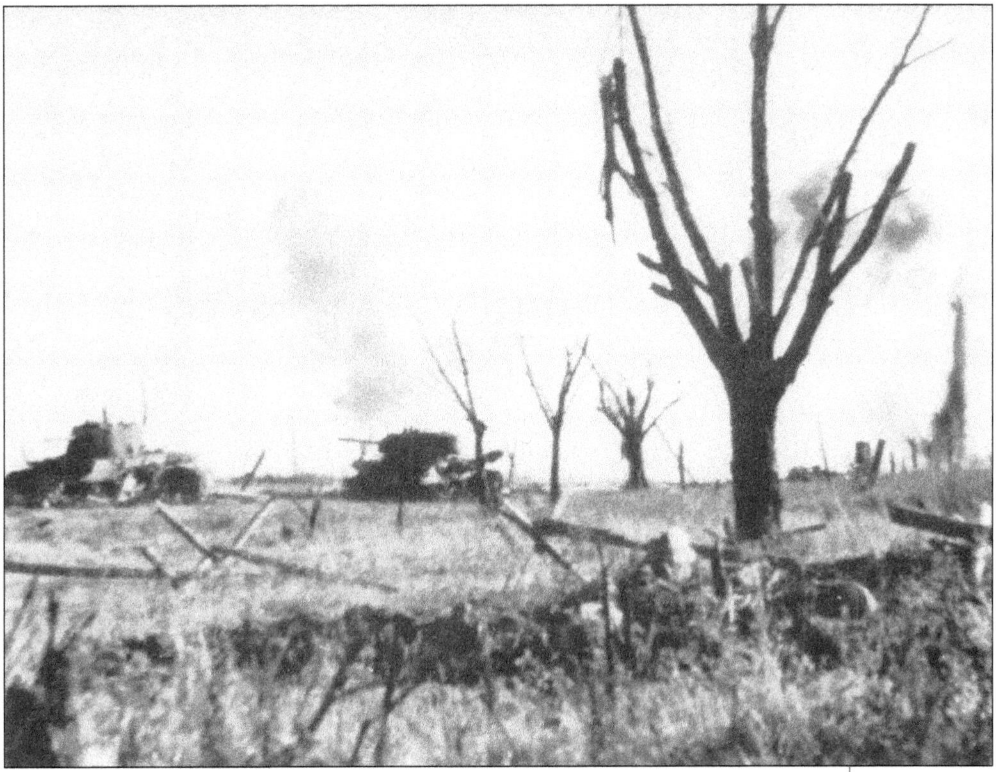

Waffen SS troops rest in a hastily made trench. The Soviet advance was so quick that it proved difficult to prepare proper defensive lines.

A *Waffen SS* sniper. Snipers worked in twos, one to look for targets and the other to take the shot.

Waffen SS troops fire an 8cm Granatwerfer 34 mortar. It was the standard German mortar used throughout the war and had a reputation for extreme accuracy and a rapid rate of fire.

A *Waffen SS* radio station command post. Unlike the start of the war German lines of communication often broke down completely during the long retreat in the East.

Standartenführer or Colonel Hermann Fegelein, commander of the *Waffen SS* cavalry brigade and later Hitler's brother-in-law through his political marriage to Eva Brauns sister Gretl. He was executed on 29th April 1945 after escaping the Reich Chancellery but being caught in civilian clothes fleeing the Soviets. Seen here talking to *Brigadeführer* or Major General Wilhelm Bittrich.

A bicycle squadron of the SS Cavalry brigade. The *Waffen SS* made extensive use of bicycles to get around the front, especially during the latter years of the war when much of their armour was destroyed.

SS cavalry charge towards the front. Horses often proved much more versatile than motorised vehicles.

Waffen SS troops carry a wounded comrade on a stretcher. One in three *Waffen SS* troops died or went missing in action during the long retreat.

In the south of the eastern front German depleted units of the *Waffen SS* Divisions "*Totenkopf*" and "*Frundsberg*", are driven back into Romania.

Waffen SS troops hitch a ride on the back of a Panzer tank. From 1944 onwards they found themselves in almost constant retreat.

In early 1944, the improved Soviet tank T-34-85 was introduced in response to the German Tiger tank, with a more powerful 85 mm gun and a three-man turret design.

Waffen SS troops shelter behind a knocked out T34 tank.

The Germans also developed new weapons. Infantrymen with an assault StG 44 carabine rifle. It could fire 500-600 rounds a minute and had an effective range of 800 metres.

An anti-tank *Jadgpanzer* 38t or "Hetzer" gun belonging to the *Waffen* SS Division *"Florian Geyer"* is brought up to the front. A light anti tank gun it was massed produced but suffered from having thin armour.

Sturmbannführer or Major Otto Skorzeny, who became famous for liberating Mussolini in July 1943, occupies the castle of Budapest. Having found out the Hungarians were negotiating a surrender with the Soviets, in a daring 'snatch' raid he kidnapped the son of Hungary's Regent, Admiral Miklós Horthy, and forced him to resign as head of state. It delayed Hungary's secession from Germany.

Soldiers of the 3rd SS-Panzer-Division *"Totenkopf"* rest and take meal break in Romania next to a destroyed Soviet tank T-34, 1944.

Waffen SS troops advance along a ditch in the fighting for Hungary, November 1944.

Due to intensive *Waffen SS* resistance Hungary was not to fall to the Soviets until the spring of 1945.

The *Waffen SS* mountain division *"Prinz Eugen"* supported by Yugoslav and Croat units were involved in heavy fighting with Tito's partisans in the hilly country of Yugoslavia.

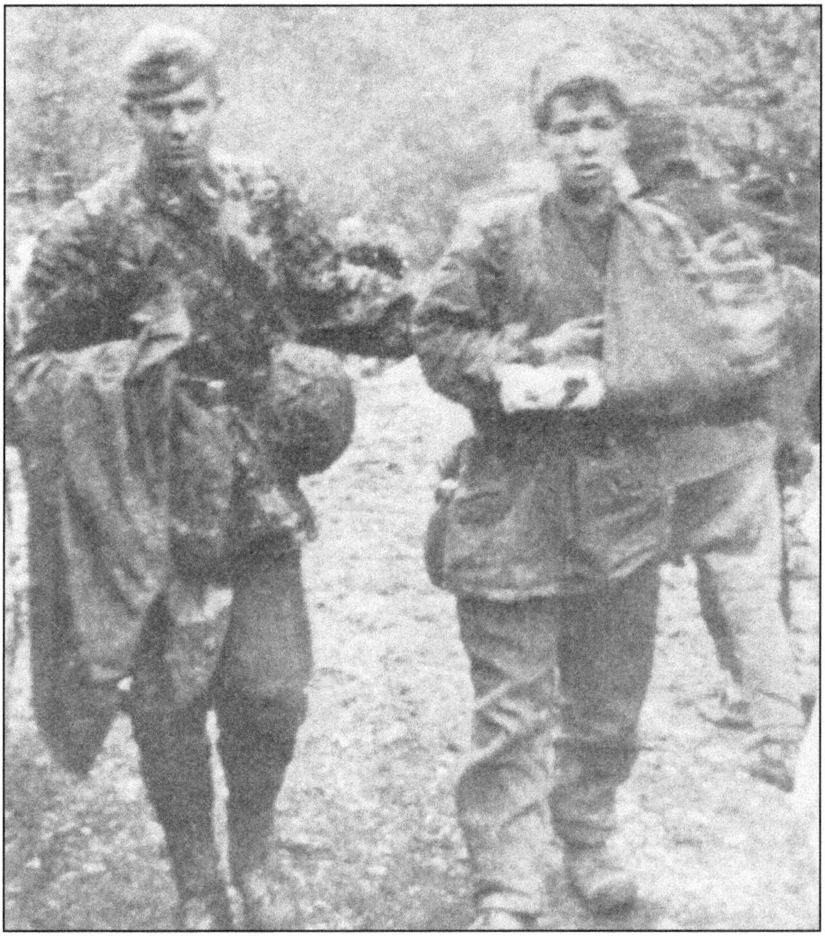

Obergruppenführer or General Artur Phleps, who was killed by Soviet troops after his capture on 21st September 1944 in Rumania, was the commanding general of the V. SS-Mountain-Corps.

Standartenführer or Colonel Otto Krumm, commander of the 7th SS Division "*Prinz Eugen*". He took part in Operation Spring Awakening (*Frühlingserwachen*) from March 6 until March 16, 1945. It was the last major German offensive launched during World War Two.

The mud splattered face of defeat on a motorcycle messenger of the *"Prinz Eugen"* Division.

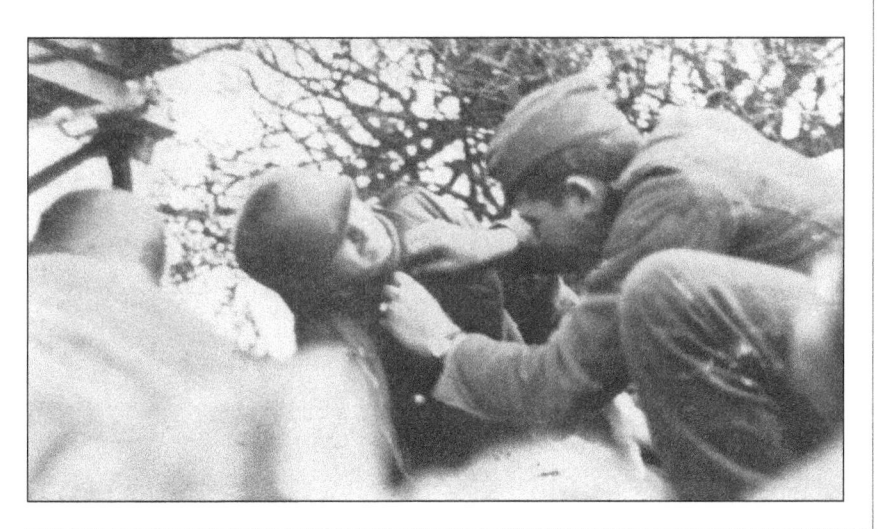

Waffen SS troops rescue an injured comrade under fire. *Waffen SS* injuries in the war in the East are not known but have been estimated at up to 400,000 men.

Waffen SS mountain Division "*Prinz Eugen*" return fire in the mountains of Yugoslavia.

In the high mountains of Yugoslavia the *Waffen SS* fought an intensive battle with Josip Broz Tito's partisans throughout 1944 and into May 1945. They were a communist lead resistance movement that in 1944 numbered over 800,000 men in 52 divisions. *Waffen SS* troops are seen here with horses and a captured French tank.

The *Waffen SS* took heavy casualties in 1944 and 1945 along the whole of the Eastern Front. Many of the later divisions were only regimental or brigade sized units who lacked the fighting spirit of the earlier ones.

The winter of 1944 was bitter meaning the Germans in retreat were fighting both the Russians and the elements.

A reconnaissance troop makes its way to the Russian line in the northern sector of the Eastern front. Unlike the *Wehrmacht* morale among *Waffen SS* remained in the main high.

On the right *Obertsturmbannführer* Hans Dorr, of the 5th SS Panzer Division "*Germania*" in the 5th SS-Pz. Division "*Wiking*". Dorr was killed in Austria in April 1945. He was injured 16 times during the war and received the Knights Cross with Oak Leaves and Swords for his bravery.

Waffen SS troops try in vain to stem the Soviet advance. By 1944 severe shortages of winter clothing meant that they had to rely on the generosity of civilians who were asked by the Nazi regime to donate furs and other winter coats.

A Hummel or "bumble-bee" self propelled artillery gun arrives at the front. It had a 15cm howitzer and was first used in the Battle of Kursk. It had a range of over 130 miles. By the end of the war over 700 had been built.

In the East the *Waffen SS* found themselves having to defend an ever collapsing German front in which the line was regularly overrun by Soviets troops.

Shortage of heavy armour and tanks in the last 6 months of the war saw *Waffen SS* troops trying to stop Russian tanks with machine guns.

Infantrymen from the regiment "*Der Führer*" await the oncoming Soviet forces.

German troops rest behind 'snow walls' in the winter of 1944 on the Eastern front. Given the speed of the Russian offensive they were often the only defensive positions they could construct.

An SS Cavalry Division officer discusses the worsening situation in the East with his troops. To the end *Waffen SS* troops carried out localised counterthrusts against the Soviet juggernaut. Meant to bring relief for a few crucial days, they often ended in failure and the death of most of those taking part.

In the closing year of the war ammunition was rationed as supply lines to the German front in the East collapsed.

A sniper targeting Russian reconnaissance troops in the northen sector of the Eastern front.

The long retreat in the East saw the Germans defending a 1400 mile front. Hopelessly outnumbered, now only the most fanatical *Waffen SS* soldiers believed they could still win and most saw their role as defending the Fatherland against Bolshevism.

As the Soviets advanced through Poland in late 1944, the German administration collapsed. Over 600,000 Soviet soldiers died fighting German troops in Poland. A Communist-controlled adminstration, headed by Bolesław Bierut, was installed by the Soviets in July in Lublin, the first major Polish city to be seized by Russia from Germany.

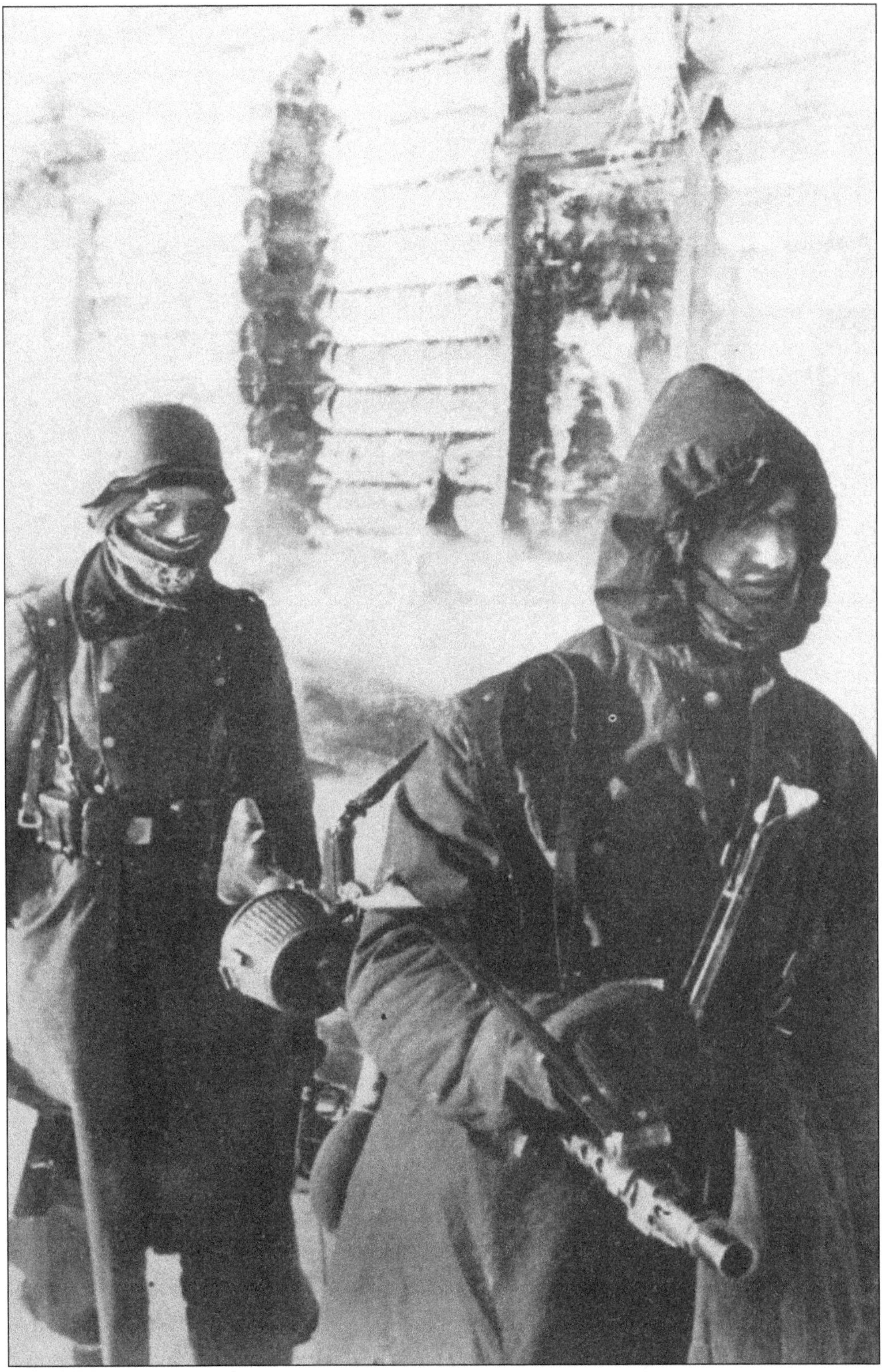

Waffen SS tanks from the 3rd Division *Totenkopf* and snipers in Poland, July 1944. After the Soviets launched Operation Bagration, the largest and last offensive to be launched from Russian soil, the SS Panzer Corps were the only line of defence after the destruction of Army Group Centre.

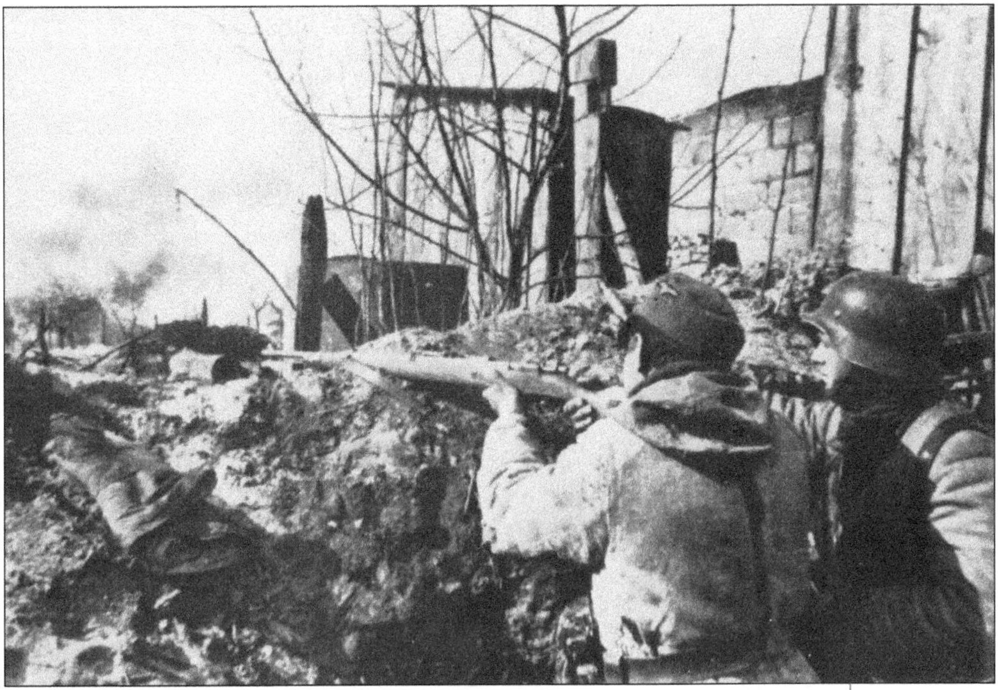

Waffen SS troops man an 88mm anti aircraft gun and retreat across a bridge in a halftrack while a knocked out German tank lies in the river. By February 1945 the whole of Poland was under Soviet control.

The *Waffen SS* in Hungary fought a more successful rearguard action, holding out until 1945. By the end of the war over 300,000 Hungarian soldiers and 80,000 civilians had died.

A *Waffen SS* infantry waits for a tram to take him to the front at Budapest. He is carrying the *Panzerfaust* or "armour fist", an anti tank bazooka. It could penetrate 200mm of armour.

A *Waffen SS* soldier uses his body as an improvised stand while another soldier fires the MG42 machine gun. By 1945 much of the *Waffen SS* armour had been destroyed.

As the Germans retreated they employed a scorched earth policy to deprive the Red Army of anything of value. However, the sheer speed of the Soviet advance often caught the Germans off guard.

Waffen SS units fought furiously in the Baltic in defence of East Prussia but the Soviets still marched into the region in January 1945, the first German state to be occupied in the East.

Obertsturmbannführer or Lieutenant Colonel Leon Degrelle during the retreat of his division to the border of the *Reich*. Commander of the 28th *Waffen SS* Division "*Walloon*" from Belgium, he was severely wounded in 1944 and was one of only three foreigners to win the Oak Leaves to the Knights Cross.

Petrol was severely rationed in the final months of the war.

When the Red Army crossed the border of the *Reich*, panic set in. A quickly dug defensive position on the outskirts of a town in Lower-Silesia.

A lack of heavy weapons meant infantrymen had to fight the Russians with "*Haftladungen*" or hand held mines.

As the fighting raged in Germany even injured *Waffen SS* troops were expected to stay on the front line.

Exhausted German troops sleep in a makeshift bunker.

Due to an almost complete breakdown in communication, messages had to be delivered to the front in person, often under heavy bombardment from the air and land.

A *Waffen SS* soldier emerges from a trench. Many of the 38 *Waffen SS* divisions were decimated by the end of the war.

As the Soviets fought their way to Berlin, German defences collapsed although some towns continued to hold out, often at huge cost to both soldiers and civilians.

Demoralised, defeated and exhausted, *Waffen SS* troops contemplate their fate at the hands of the Soviets.

A *Waffen SS* soldier loads a 30mm *Schießbecher* or "shooting cup" grenade onto his K98 rifle. It was effective against infantry, fortifications and light armoured vehicles up to a range of 280 m.

As the Soviets advanced through Germany *Waffen SS* resistance intensified but with a huge numerical supremacy in men and material the final outcome was never in doubt.

Units of the *Waffen SS* defend the town of Küstrin. The unexpected arrival of Soviet troops at the end of January 1945 at the ancient fortress and garrison town came as a tremendous shock to the German High Command - the Soviets were now only 50 miles from Berlin itself. Two Soviet armies lay siege to the town. Despite this the Germans held out for 60 days but at an appalling human cost - about 5,000 Germans were killed, 9,000 wounded and 6,000 captured. The Russians lost 5,000 killed and 15,000 wounded.

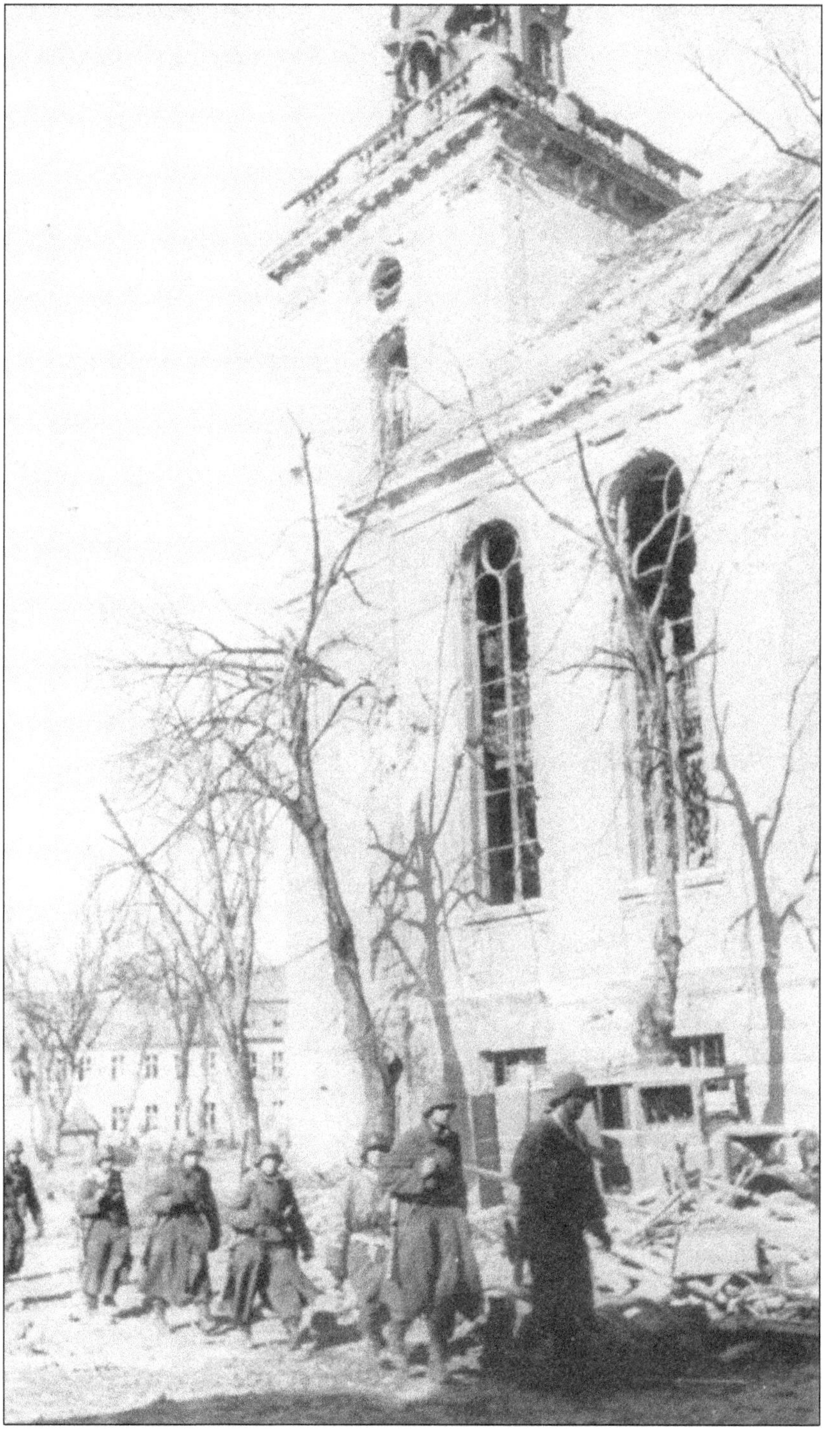

The Battle of Berlin was the last major offensive battle in the East. Intensive street battles left much of the city in ruins. In the defence of Berlin over 100,000 German soldiers were killed before Hitler committed suicide on 30 April 1945. Over 125,000 civilians also died in the battle.

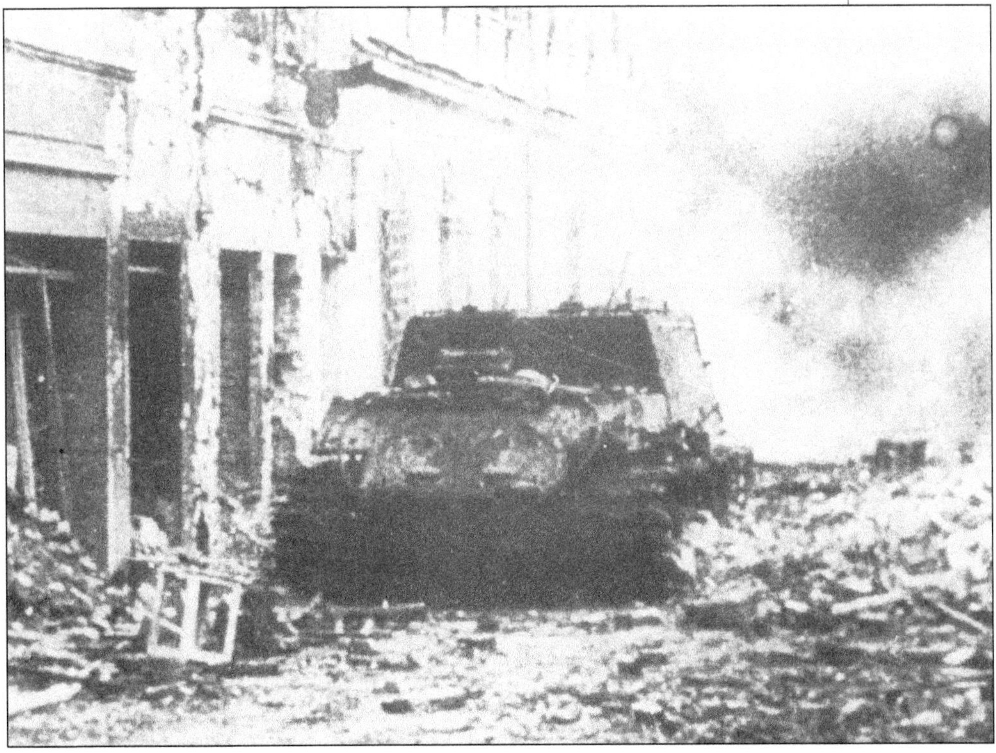

Most of the *Waffen SS* soldiers killed in the East were buried in foreign soil with no grave marker.

The last days and hours of the war saw many *Waffen SS* soldiers head westwards to avoid capture by the Soviets.

Waffen SS troops surrendering to US troops.

Brigadeführer or Major General Jürgen Wagner hands his unit over to US-troops. Commander of the 23rd SS Division *Nederland* and later the 4th Polizei Division he was awarded the Oak Leaves Knights Cross with Oak Leaves for bravery in December 1944. He was executed in 1947 by the Yugoslav Army for war crimes.

Reporters from the *Waffen SS* took many photos during the war including most of those in this book but they were heavily censored to show the divisions only engaging in heroic struggles and hiding the dreadful cost of war.

After hostilities had finally ceased on 8 May 1945 nearly one in three *Waffen SS* troops were dead or missing in action. To put their mortality rate in context it was the equivalent of all the casualties suffered by the United States military during the entire war.

ABOUT CODA BOOKS

Most Coda books are edited and endorsed by Emmy Award winning film make and military historian Bob Carruthers, producer of Discovery Channel's Line of Fire and Weapons of War and BBC's Both Sides of the Line. Long experience and strong editorial control gives the military history enthusiast the ability to but with confidence. The series advisor is David McWhinnie, producer of the acclaimed Battlefield series for Discovery Channel. David and Bob have co-produced books and films with a wide variety of the UK's leading historians including Professor John Erickson and Dr. David Chandler. Where possible the books draw on rare primary sources to give the miliary enthusiast new insights into a fascinating subject.

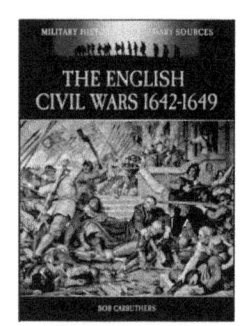

The English Civil Wars	The Zulu Wars	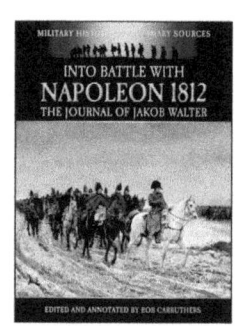 Into Battle with Napoleon 1812	Waterloo 1815
The Anglo-Saxon Chronicle	 The Battle of the Bulge	The Normandy Campaign 1944	Hitler's Justification for WWII
 Hitler's Mein Kampf - The Roots of Evil	I Knew Hitler	 Mein Kampf - The 1939 Illustrated Edition	The Nuremberg Trials Volume 1

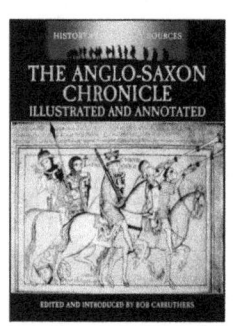

www.codahistory.com

Tiger I in Combat	Tiger I Crew Manual	Panzers at War 1939-1942	Panzers at War 1943-1945
Wolf Pack - the U boats	Poland 1939	Luftwaffe Combat Reports	Eastern Front Night Combat
Eastern Front Encirclement	Panzer Combat Reports	The Panther V in Combat	The Red Army in Combat
Barbarossa - Hitler Turns East	The Russian Front	The Wehrmacht in Russia	Servants of Evil